Published by Neil Wilson Publishing Ltd
303a The Pentagon Centre
36 Washington St
Glasgow G3 8AZ
Scotland
Tel: 0141-221-1117
Fax: 0141-221-5363

First edition published in July 1986.
Second edition published June 1987.
Reprinted August 1987, January 1988, October 1988
Third edition published September 1989.
Reprinted June, September 1990
Fourth edition published April 1991.
Reprinted August, November 1991, March 1992.
Fifth edition published November 1992.
Reprinted March 1993, December 1993, April 1994, March 1995
This edition published November 1995

The moral right of the author has been asserted.
A catalogue record for this book is available from the British Library
ISBN 1-897784-26-0

Edited by Neil Wilson

Typeset in 8/10pt Perpetua by The Write Stuff, Glasgow
Tel: 0141-339-8279
E-mail: *wilson_i@cqm.co.uk*

Printed by Oriental Press

Contents

Acknowledgements

Once again I express my most sincere thanks to everyone in the Scotch (and Irish!) whisk(e)y industry who have helped with the production of this new edition. Without their help, this publication would simply not exist. — WM Neil Wilson Publishing Ltd gratefully acknowledges the assistance of The Keepers of the Quaich in the production of this work.

USEFUL ADDRESSES

The Scotch Whisky Association

17 Half Moon Street

LONDON W1

Tel: 0171-629-4384

Permanent displays on the workings of a distillery with models and audio-visual. Admission free.

The Scotch Whisky Heritage Centre

354 Castlehill

The Royal Mile

EDINBURGH EH1 2NE

Tel: 0131-220-0441

Fax: 0131-220-6288

Adult admission £3.80, concessionary rates available. Audio-visual guided tours, gift shop. Open all year, seven days a week.

Foreword

It is always pleasant to pay tribute to a thoroughly deserving publication, in this case *The Malt Whisky Almanac* by Wallace Milroy. The Keepers of the Quaich are delighted to be associated with this present edition which will help to stimulate discussion and experimentation leading to one of life's great pleasures — the tasting and appreciation of Scotland's malt whiskies. The fellowship of those who enjoy Scotland and her whiskies is ever expanding and I have no doubt that this almanac will further the good work.

The Earl of Mansfield, D.L., J.P.

Introduction

As I write this introduction exports of Scotch whisky have reached the record value of £2,191 million. This extraordinary performance, up almost 5% from last year, has been managed despite a 2% decrease in volume to 252.21 million litres of pure alcohol. That equates to about 900 million bottles which account for 87% of the total market for Scotch!

However, sales in the UK continue to languish, just as they do in the USA and Japan. So who is making up the difference and helping distillers to reach these marvellous figures? Step forward the whisky lovers of Spain, Greece, Italy and Portugal where our national drink is being received as never before. Why? The simple reason is tax. Due to the favourable taxation of Scotch in the southern states of the EU, Spain has shot past France as the second most valuable market for Scotch with exports worth £205 million entering the country. Greece was up 11% to £92 million and the Portuguese imported some £55 million worth of Scotch, up by 17%. Italy, where malt is a revered luxury, was up 22% to £72 million. Not counting the UK, the EU states contributed 37% of Scotch exports and given that sales to the USA are stagnant at £283 million, the rise in popularity in the Mediterranean countries has been of great relief.

But the industry is not getting a fair chance to compete in the UK where discriminatory taxation hits sales hard. The Chancellor's last budget increase of 26p per bottle has only fuelled the problem. Since the beginning of January this year, sales of Scotch in the UK have slipped by 26% resulting in losses of some £100 million to the Exchequer if the trend continues throughout the year. There is another trend, however, of consumers enjoying smaller quantities of higher quality Scotch. The malt sector has again confounded analysts with a 20% rise in consumption and the public is now enjoying an ever-increasing array of bottlings, some from distillers who have been averse to extending their retail portfolio in the past.

The Scotch Whisky Association will continue to press Brussels for tax equalisation throughout the European Community in order to allow our national drink the 'level playing field' it requires, but I fear that for some

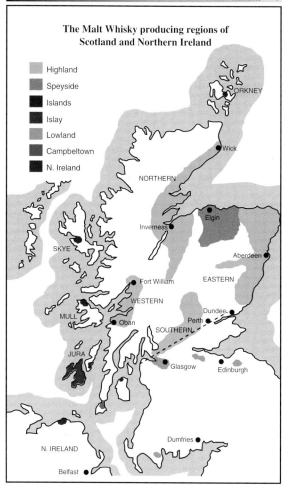

The Malt Whisky producing regions of Scotland and Northern Ireland

- Highland
- Speyside
- Islands
- Islay
- Lowland
- Campbeltown
- N. Ireland

ORKNEY

Wick

NORTHERN

Elgin

Inverness

Aberdeen

SKYE

EASTERN

Fort William

WESTERN

Dundee.

MULL

Oban

Perth

SOUTHERN

JURA

Glasgow

Edinburgh

Dumfries

N. IRELAND

Belfast

time to come Britons will continue to return from their summer holidays in the sun, unable to comprehend why their bottle of Scotch costs more at home than abroad. And so long as the Chancellor continues to allow imported wines and beers to be taxed less than home-produced spirits, the situation will remain.

But this book is all about the enjoyment of drinking good malt whisky, even if it is an expensive commodity! A new edition allows my publisher full scope to revise, update, renew and rewrite and with 16 more pages in full colour, still in handy format, this pocket guide is better than ever. Furthermore I have added distillery information which includes the manager's name at the time of writing, the number of wash and spirit stills (a good indication of the relative size of each distillery), the type of cask woods used for maturation (where available), full tel/fax details, disabled access to reception centres and audio visual, gift shop and tasting facilities.

Distilleries which no longer exist, or which are unlikely to reopen, have now been removed from the main section in the book and allocated a section of their own, Lost Distilleries on page 133. Their product is only available on a limited basis and it is best to scour the specialist shops or check with the independent bottlers when trying to trace a bottle (see pages 153–155). It is regrettable that the number of distilleries appearing in this part of the book now number almost 20. The only positive sign regarding this decline is the establishment of some new distilleries in the past couple of years such as Kininvie, Speyside and the Arran Distillery which will be officially opened as this book goes to press.

With so many vintage and cask strength bottlings now on the market, the variety of labels is far greater than before and in some cases we have reproduced a few of the more unusual ones. Another development is that I have given our friends in Northern Ireland a chapter of their own in order to give the reader a greater insight into the local development of the industry and their unique product. In the past Ulster was much more involved in whiskey-making and I have expanded on this theme. If there is a moral in this, it might be that you should take each and every opportunity to taste whichever malt comes your way since a distillery closed, is a malt lost forever, but a bottle found from the same distillery is a golden opportunity to savour a piece of history.

Finally, please refer to the symbols listed opposite when checking distillery entries. We have used these to save space, simplify the information given and to help foreign visitors who have not. as yet, had a chance to buy this book in their own language.

Wallace Milroy
London, June, 1995

KEY TO SYMBOLS

Address

Telephone number

Fax number

Reception Centre

Audio-visual

Disabled access

Restricted disabled access

Gift shop

Tastings

Number of wash stills

Number of spirit stills

Cask woods used for maturation

Type of maltings

ABBREVIATIONS

IWSC   International Wine and Spirit Competition

ROSPA Royal Society for the Prevention of Accidents

ASVA   Association of Scottish Visitor Attractions

Visiting distilleries

For many visitors to Scotland a trip to Edinburgh Castle or the Burrell Collection in Glasgow is considered a must. Now, however, a trip to visit a whisky distillery is viewed by many as being just as essential and many of the producers have established high quality venues to entertain and educate this growing band of overseas enthusiasts who want to witness malt whisky being made at source. It seems that no matter where a distillery is situated, people make an effort to visit.

Many of these distilleries have received a great deal of investment in order to cope with the seasonal influx of visitors, whereas some of the remoter plants simply get by with a welcome dram, a small exhibition and a few seats in a side-room. In both cases, the sincerity of the welcome is equally heartfelt, so don't be put off by what appears to be a lack of facilities. The staff of Scotland's distilleries are always keen to promote their own dram. For example, the remote Islay distillery, Caol Ila, so magnificently situated on the Sound of Islay, is dealing with about 2,000 visitors a year; Scotland's highest distillery at Dalwhinnie is drawing 40,000 visitors off the A9 each year and Oban in the west is coping with some 35,000 per annum. At the other end of the scale, Glenturret near Crieff catered for 215,000 in the last year and the marvellous new Heritage Centre at Strathisla in Keith is set to become one of the major attractions in Speyside.

Another major point of interest for the enthusiast is Speyside Cooperage (tel: 01340-881264, fax: 01340-881303) which is on the Speyside Malt Whisky Trail and can be found on the Dufftown Road, Craigellachie, AB38 9RS. It is open from Easter to the end of September, Monday to Saturday from 09.30 to 16.30 and from October to the end of March from 09.30 to 16.30. It is closed for the two weeks over Christmas and New Year. Admission is £1.70 for adults and £1.20 for children and concessions. Family tickets are £4.90 and groups of 15 or more can book in for £1.10 per head. Well worth a visit.

In this chapter, I have set out on a regional basis those companies and distilleries which offer facilities, further details of which can be found under the actual distillery entries. Distilleries which are the Malt Whisky Trail are marked with an asterisk.

ALLIED DISTILLERS

A company much transformed in recent years, and now tied up with the Spanish Domecq group, Allied have yet to invest as heavily in visitor reception centres as some of their competitors.

Region	Distillery	Page No
Speyside	Glendronach	39
Eastern Highlands	Glencadam	83
Islay	Laphroaig	115

BEN NEVIS DISTILLERY (Fort William) Ltd

Japanese ownership has seen an investment made in this west-coast reception centre which has resulted in some 40,000 visitors stopping off at the distillery last year.

Region	Distillery	Page No
Western Highlands	Ben Nevis	95

BURN STEWART DISTILLERS PLC

The recent purchase of Tobermory Distillery has been viewed positively in the island of Mull and should bring in a far greater number of visitors to what is a wonderfully situated location at the entry to the harbour in the village.

Region	Distillery	Page No
Islands	Tobermory	129

CAMPBELL DISTILLERS LTD

This French-owned company has successfully exploited Edradour's unique character in being Scotland's smallest distillery and they have actively promoted Aberlour in France.

Region	Distillery	Page No
Speyside	Aberlour	17
Southern Highlands	Edradour	89

THE CHIVAS & GLENLIVET DIVISION
THE SEAGRAM COMPANY

With their five-year Heritage Programme under way, the Chivas & Glenlivet Group are now focusing their efforts around their Speyside distilling operations and undertaking restoration and development work on projects directly related to the whisky-making traditions of the area. In the words of their President, James Espey, the programme 'demonstrates not only genuine long-term commitment to our outstanding brand portfolio, but also to Scotland's past heritage and future success'. The result of this has been dramatic with the development of the Heritage Centre at Strathisla, the restoration of Linn House in Keith and the Glen Grant Gardens at the distillery in Rothes.

Region	Distillery	Page No
Speyside	Glen Keith	34
	Glen Grant*	33
	Glenlivet*	45
	Strathisla*	62

THE HIGHLAND DISTILLERIES CO PLC

The mergers and acquisitions of the last few years have extended the number of distilleries in this company's portfolio, but only two reception centres are currently operating, albeit with one of them at Glenturret, possibly the busiest of all in Scotland.

Region	Distillery	Page No
Southern Highlands	Glenturret	91
Islands	Highland Park	125

HISTORIC SCOTLAND

Not a producer as such, but Historic Scotland have a 30-year tenure of one of Scotland's distilleries and are therefore very much involved in promoting the heritage of the industry. The distillery in their care is perfectly preserved and is now a protected monument. Despite its lack of industry, it is still a worthwhile stop if you are in the area.

Region	Distillery	Page No
Speyside	Dallas Dhu*	30

THE MACALLAN-GLENLIVET DISTILLERS PLC

With only one distillery in the company's portfolio, this firm has invested wisely in their HQ building at Easter Elchies, Craigellachie and if you are one of the lucky ones able to sample this wonderful whisky in its own setting, you will not be disappointed.

Region	Distillery	Page No
Speyside	Macallan	55

ISLE OF ARRAN DISTILLERS LTD

A brand-new visitors' centre which is expected to draw 100,000 visitors has just opened at Lochranza where the newest addition to Scotland's distillery portfolio is now on stream. Although it will be a few years before the cratur is matured and ready, the distillery is fully functional in all other respects.

Region	Distillery	Page No
Islands	Arran	124

J & G GRANT

One of the essential stops when visiting Speyside, if only for the fact that this is still a family-owned business and likely to remain so.

Region	Distillery	Page No
Speyside	Glenfarclas*	42

IRISH DISTILLERS LTD

Now wholly French-owned but very definitely remaining Irish in spirit, the company continues to offer visitors to their Old Bushmills Distillery on the beautiful Co Antrim coast a very rewarding time at the UK's oldest licensed distillery.

Region	Distillery	Page No
Northern Ireland	Old Bushmills	131

LANG BROS LTD

Closely associated with Highland Distilleries, this long-established company manages what is perhaps the best distillery to visit while in the Glasgow area, if only for its location beneath the Campsie Fells. The facilities will probably be available all year round from now on.

Region	Distillery	Page No
Southern Highlands	Glengoyne	90

MACDONALD MARTIN DISTILLERIES PLC

Their famous '16 men of Tain' advertising campaign has paid dividends in terms of cachet for this Leith-based distiller (soon to move out to Broxburn), and their distillery situated in a beautiful part of Easter Ross should not be missed out.

Region	Distillery	Page No
Northern Highlands	Glenmorangie	76

MORRISON BOWMORE DISTILLERS LTD

Now concentrating solely on their Islay distillery, this Japanese-owned company has recently upgraded the retail facilities and offer a very complete experience for the visitor. Although Islay remains relatively remote in terms of road and ferry access, remember that it is only a 30-minute flight from Glasgow.

Region	Distillery	Page No
Islay	Bowmore	109

TAKARA SHUZO & OKURA & CO LTD

A gradual development of facilities over the past few years at this company's one Scottish distillery has brought a significant increase in the number of visitors who want to have a look at one of the largest distilleries in Scotland.

Region	Distillery	Page No
Northern Highlands	Tomatin	80

UNITED DISTILLERS

This company is Scotland's largest producer of malt whisky and has developed an extensive number of visitor centres throughout Scotland. A great deal of investment has gone into these and they are now amongst the best.

Region	Distillery	Page No
Speyside	Cardhu*	26
	Cragganmore	27
Northern Highlands	Clynelish	71
	Dalwhinnie	73
	Glen Ord	75
Eastern Highlands	Royal Lochnagar	85
Southern Highlands	Aberfeldy	86
	Blair Athol	87
Western Highlands	Oban	96
Lowlands	Glenkinchie	101
Islay	Lagavulin	114
Islands	Talisker	128

THE WHYTE & MACKAY GROUP PLC

This Glasgow-based, American-owned company has always concentrated on their one reception facility in the east and have no plans to extend their investment to any of their other distilleries at present.

Region	Distillery	Page No
Eastern Highlands	Fettercairn	84

WM GRANT & SONS LTD

Although now operating three distilleries within Dufftown, one well-developed reception centre services all the company's requirements. It is largely based around the Glenfiddich experience, with Kininvie and Balvenie remaining a little in the background. Dufftown is one of the best places to visit to appreciate the scale of distilling in Scotland when the late-Victorian boom occurred.

Region	Distillery	Page No
Speyside	Glenfiddich*	43

Speyside

For many whisky enthusiasts malt whisky is most closely associated with Speyside, but in truth this is only half the story. The strength of the association, however, can be seen from the many distilleries which, although not situated beside the River Spey, make allegiance with it when stating their provenance.

The River Livet has also suffered from the same back-handed compliment and over the years many distillers (even true Speyside producers) claimed to produce 'a Glenlivet', when strictly speaking they were stretching not only the geographical boundaries a bit far, but also the patience of the owners of The Glenlivet Distillery itself. It all goes to show how over the last two centuries 'Speyside' has meant high quality, and today the truth of that statement has not diminished at all.

The trade, however, has always tended to look at the large number of distilleries situated in this area as simply 'Speysides', and for simplicity's sake I have continued with this categorisation for this sixth edition. As you will see from the accompanying map, the 'Golden Triangle' really exists, stretching from Elgin over towards Banff and down to the cradle of distilling on Speyside — Dufftown. In this triangle lies the greatest concentration of malt whisky-making apparatus in the world, and to savour the atmosphere here is to realise how important and how dearly distilling is held in the Highlands of Scotland.

The success of the Speyside distillers and their current profusion is due to the production of illicit whisky. At the end of the 18th century, the Highland product was in such demand that the 'protected' Lowland markets were infiltrated with the higher quality, smuggled produce of the illicit still. Finally, in 1823, an Act of Parliament betrayed the fact that the Government had at last realised the best way to reduce the illicit trade was to make it attractive for the distillers to go legal. The Speyside men were, however, suspicious and only after George Smith, who distilled in Glenlivet, went legal in 1824 did they begin to accept the new laws.

Smith's foresight is manifested in the industry on Speyside as it stands today where over 40 malt distilleries are in operation.

Perhaps the most positive development in recent years has been the

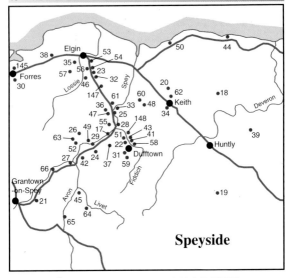

DISTILLERY LOCATION NUMBERS REFER TO PAGE NUMBERS

development of new distilleries and the sale of others within the industry. Within the Seagram portfolio, Allt a'Bhainne and Braes of Glenlivet have been established for some years, although I have yet to sample their produce which is used solely for blending, and I have therefore given no distillery or tastings details on them. Similarly Strathmill, whilst established in 1891, is used for fillings by Justerini & Brooks and is therefore not listed. Kininvie at Dufftown has been producing for a few years but I have yet to sample its wares. Hopefully it won't be too long before we see distilleries which have changed hands beginning to produce again. The Benromach site (see page 145) was recently sold to Gordon & Macphail who are re-equipping it for future production, so here's hoping.

BRAND	**Aberlour**
DISTILLERY	Aberlour
	ABERLOUR, Banffshire AB38 9PJ
	01340-871204/285
	01340-871729
MANAGER	Alan J. Winchester
OWNING COMPANY	Campbell Distillers Ltd
PRODUCTION STATUS	Operational
ESTABLISHED	1826, rebuilt 1880
SOURCE	Private springs on Ben Rinnes
	2 2

	01340-871204/01340-871285
	01340-871729
	Tours twice weekly, Tue & Fri: 10.00 & 16.00.
VISITORS PER ANNUM	1000

AGE WHEN BOTTLED	10 years
STRENGTH	40 & 57.1%
SPECIAL BOTTLINGS	1969, 1970 vintages.
EXPORT BOTTLINGS	'Antique' @ 43%

TASTING NOTES	10 years, 40%
NOSE	Rich, malty aroma.
TASTE	A hint of smoke on the palate with a restrained sweetness.
COMMENTS	Increasingly popular after-dinner dram now in French ownership (Pernod-Ricard). A well-balanced Speyside in which many have invested in a personal bottling for the year 2000!

BRAND	**An Cnoc**
DISTILLERY	Knockdhu
	📠 KNOCK, Aberdeenshire AB5 5LJ
	📞 01466-771223 📠 01466-771359
MANAGER	Stanley Harrower
OWNING COMPANY	Knockdhu Distillery Co., Ltd.
PRODUCTION STATUS	Operational
ESTABLISHED	1893-4
SOURCE	Five springs on the Knock Hill

AGE WHEN BOTTLED	12 years
STRENGTH	40%

TASTING NOTES	
NOSE	A distinctive soft aroma with a hint of smoke.
TASTE	Very refined with a mellow smooth, mild softness and a long finish.
COMMENTS	An excellent all round malt. This distillery was the first bought by The Distillers Co to supply malt whisky for their own use. This malt was previously marketed as Knockdhu.

MALT	**Ardmore**
DISTILLERY	Ardmore
	📧 KENNETHMONT
	Aberdeenshire AB54 4NH
	☎ 01464-831213 📠 01464-831428
MANAGER	Mr J Sim
OWNING COMPANY	Allied Distillers Ltd
PRODUCTION STATUS	Operational
ESTABLISHED	1898
SOURCE	Springs on Knockandy Hill
	🌾 4 🛢 4

TASTING NOTES	1981, 40%
NOSE	A light aroma.
TASTE	Big, sweet and malty on the palate with a good, crisp finish.
COMMENTS	After-dinner dram. A limited edition bottling is sometimes available from Wm Teacher at 15 years and 45.7%. See also page 153.

SPEYSIDE
SINGLE MALT *SCOTCH WHISKY*

AULTMORE

distillery located between KEITH and BUCKIE began production in 1897. The name, derived from the Gaelic, means 'big burn'. Ideal supplies of water and peat from the Foggie Moss made this once a haunt of illicit distillers in the past. Water from the Burn of AUCHINDERRAN is now used to produce this smooth, well balanced single MALT SCOTCH WHISKY with a mellow finish.

AGED **12** YEARS

43% vol Distilled & Bottled in SCOTLAND, AULTMORE DISTILLERY, Keith, Banffshire, Scotland 70cl

BRAND	**Aultmore**
DISTILLERY	Aultmore
	KEITH, Banffshire AB55 3QY
	01542-882762 01542-886467
MANAGER	Jim Riddell
OWNING COMPANY	United Distillers
PRODUCTION STATUS	Operational
ESTABLISHED	1897
SOURCE	Auchinderran Burn
	2 2

AGE WHEN BOTTLED	12 years
STRENGTH	43%

TASTING NOTES	
NOSE	A delightful, fresh aroma with a sweet hint and a touch of peat.
TASTE	Smooth, well-balanced with a mellow, warming finish.
COMMENTS	Now generally available as a brand and suitable as an after-dinner malt.

SPEYSIDE
SINGLE MALT
SCOTCH WHISKY

Sometime in the early 19th, after walking
in the CROMDALE hills with
his 2 BROTHERS, James McGregor settled
and established

BALMENACH

distillery. Spring water from beneath these
same HILLS is still used to produce
this RICH flavoured single MALT SCOTCH
WHISKY of exemplary quality.

AGED **12** YEARS

43% vol   70cl

BRAND	**Balmenach**
DISTILLERY	Balmenach
	Cromdale, GRANTOWN-ON-SPEY
	Morayshire PH26 3PF
	01479-872569
MANAGER	Mike Gunn
OWNING COMPANY	United Distillers
PRODUCTION STATUS	Mothballed 1993
ESTABLISHED	c1824
SOURCE	Cromdale Burn
	3 3

AGE WHEN BOTTLED	12 years
STRENGTH	43%

TASTING NOTES	
NOSE	Light, attractive, sweet, nutty aroma with floral overtones and a slight hint of smoke.
TASTE	Starts quite full and firm, then lingers softly with a sweet, nutty, vanilla finish.
COMMENTS	An extremely well-balanced and satisfying drink.

BRAND	# The Balvenie
DISTILLERY	Balvenie
	🖃 Dufftown, KEITH, Banffshire AB55 4DH
	☎ 01340-820373 📠 01340-820805
MANAGER	Bill White
OWNING COMPANY	Wm Grant & Sons Ltd
PRODUCTION STATUS	Operational
ESTABLISHED	1892
SOURCE	The Robbie Dubh springs
	🛢 Ex-bourbon & sherry
	🍶 4 🍶 4
	⛲ Floor maltings

AGE WHEN BOTTLED	Founder's Reserve — 10 years
STRENGTH	Founder's Reserve, Double Wood — 40%;
	Single Barrel — 50.4%
SPECIAL BOTTLINGS	Double Wood — 12 years;
	Single Barrel — 15 years

TASTING NOTES	12-year-old, Double Wood
NOSE	Excellent well-pronounced aroma.
TASTE	Big, distinctive flavour. Almost a liqueur and a very distinct sweet aftertaste.
COMMENTS	A connoisseur's malt for after-dinner. The Double Wood is matured in two types of wood: traditional oak and then sherried oak. The Single Barrel is a single distillation bottled from a single cask, forming a limited edition of no more than 300 hand-numbered bottles.

BENRIACH DISTILLERY
EST.1898
A SINGLE
PURE HIGHLAND MALT
Scotch Whisky
Benriach Distillery, in the heart of the Highlands,
still malts its own barley. The resulting whisky has
a unique and attractive delicacy
PRODUCED AND BOTTLED BY THE
BENRIACH
DISTILLERY CO
ELGIN, MORAYSHIRE, SCOTLAND, IV30 3SJ
Distilled and Bottled in Scotland
AGED 10 YEARS
70cl e 43%vol

BRAND	**Benriach**
DISTILLERY	Benriach
	▣ Longmorn, ELGIN, Morayshire IV30 3SJ
	☎ 01542-783400 🖶 01542-783404
MANAGER	Bob MacPherson
OWNING COMPANY	The Seagram Co Ltd
PRODUCTION STATUS	Operational
ESTABLISHED	1898. Closed 1900. Re-established 1965.
SOURCE	Local springs
	🍶 2 🍶 2
	♨ Floor maltings

AGE WHEN BOTTLED	10 years
STRENGTH	43%

TASTING NOTES	
NOSE	Light, sweet and delicate with a hint of fruit.
TASTE	Medium-bodied yet complex with a combined delicacy of flowering currants and peat. Delicate, dry, refined aftertaste.
COMMENTS	A 'Heritage Selection' malt from Chivas, now repackaged

BRAND	**Benrinnes**
DISTILLERY	Benrinnes
	ABERLOUR, Banffshire AB38 9NN
	01340-871215 01340-871840
MANAGER	Neil Gillies
OWNING COMPANY	United Distillers
PRODUCTION STATUS	Operational
ESTABLISHED	c1835
SOURCE	Rowantree and Scurran Burns
	2 4
AWARDS RECEIVED	ROSPA Health & Safety Gold Award 1994

AGE WHEN BOTTLED	15 years
STRENGTH	43%

TASTING NOTES

NOSE	A delightful, sweet and flowery aroma.
TASTE	Firm, positive with a hint of blackberry fruitiness. It has a liqueur-like quality with a clean, fresh taste which lingers.
COMMENTS	An excellent after-dinner dram.

MALT	**Caperdronich**
DISTILLERY	Caperdonich
	🖳 ROTHES, Morayshire AB38 7BS
	☎ 01542-783300
MANAGER	Willie Mearns
OWNING COMPANY	The Seagram Co Ltd
PRODUCTION STATUS	Operational
ESTABLISHED	1898. Closed 1902. Re-established 1965.
SOURCE	The Caperdonich Burn
	🜪 2 🜪 2

TASTING NOTES	14-year-old, 46%
NOSE	A light, very delicate fragrance of peat.
TASTE	Medium, slight hint of fruit with a quick smoky finish.
COMMENTS	The distillery is across the road from Glen Grant and used to be called Glen Grant No 2. A pre-dinner dram, see page 154.

BRAND	**Cardhu**
	(Kaar-doo)
DISTILLERY	Cardhu
	Knockando, ABERLOUR
	Banffshire AB38 7RY
	01340-810204 01340-810491
MANAGER	Charlie Smith
OWNING COMPANY	United Distillers
PRODUCTION STATUS	Operational
ESTABLISHED	1824
SOURCE	Springs on the Mannoch Hill and the Lyne Burn
	3 3

	01340-810204 01340-810491
	Jan-Dec, Mon-Fri: 09.30-16.30.
	May-Sept, Sat: 09.30-16.30
OTHER ATTRACTIONS	Coffee room, conference room, exhibition and picnic area
AWARDS RECEIVED	Loo of the Year, 1992!
VISITORS PER ANNUM	16,000

AGE WHEN BOTTLED	12 years
STRENGTH	40%

TASTING NOTES	
NOSE	A hint of sweetness with an excellent bouquet.
TASTE	Smooth, mellow flavour with a delightful long-lasting finish.
COMMENTS	Good after dinner dram, and a malt which is now one of United Distillers' most prominent and popular.

BRAND	**Cragganmore**
DISTILLERY	Cragganmore
	BALLINDALLOCH, Banffshire, AB37 9AB
	01807-500202 01807-500288
MANAGER	Mike Gunn
OWNING COMPANY	United Distillers
PRODUCTION STATUS	Operational
ESTABLISHED	1869
SOURCE	The Craggan Burn
	2 2

01807-500202 01807-500288
Trade visitors only.

VISITORS PER ANNUM	1000

AGE WHEN BOTTLED	12 years
STRENGTH	40%

TASTING NOTES

NOSE	Light, delicate honey nose.
TASTE	A refined, well-balanced distillate. Quite firm with a malty, smoky taste which finishes quickly.
COMMENTS	One of United Distillers' Classic Malt range.

SPEYSIDE
SINGLE MALT
SCOTCH WHISKY

CRAIGELLACHIE

*distillery, founded in 1888, in the county of
BANFFSHIRE. It stands overlooking the
RIVER SPEY, the rock of Craigellachie, and
TELFORD'S single span iron BRIDGE. The
distillery uses local spring water running from
little CONVAL HILL for mashing, resulting
in this excellent single MALT SCOTCH
WHISKY of light and smoky character.*

AGED **14** YEARS

43% vol   70cl

BRAND	**Craigellachie**
DISTILLERY	Craigellachie
	Craigellachie, ABERLOUR
	Banffshire AB38 9ST
	01340-881212/881228
	01340-881311
MANAGER	Archie Ness
OWNING COMPANY	United Distillers
PRODUCTION STATUS	Operational
ESTABLISHED	1891
SOURCE	Little Conval hill
	2 2

- -

AGE WHEN BOTTLED	14 years
STRENGTH	43%

- -

TASTING NOTES	
NOSE	Pungent, smoky.
TASTE	Light-bodied, smoky flavour. More delicate on the palate than the nose suggests. Good character.
COMMENTS	An interesting after-dinner dram.

BRAND	**Dailuaine**
	(Dale-yooin)
DISTILLERY	Dailuaine
	Carron, ABERLOUR, Banffshire AB38 7RE
	01340-810361 01340-810510
MANAGER	Neil Gillies
OWNING COMPANY	United Distillers
PRODUCTION STATUS	Operational
ESTABLISHED	c1852
SOURCE	Bailliemullich Burn
	3 3

AGE WHEN BOTTLED	16 years
STRENGTH	43%

TASTING NOTES	
NOSE	Mild sweetness with hints of smoke. Touches of honeysuckle against an oaky background.
TASTE	Full flavoured with a malt presence enhancing the rich, dry, sweet, refreshing finish.
COMMENTS	An excellent all-round dram.

BRAND	**Dallas Dhu**
DISTILLERY	Dallas Dhu
	FORRES, Morayshire IV36 0RR
OWNING COMPANY	United Distillers
PRODUCTION STATUS	Closed 1983. Can be re-instated
ESTABLISHED	1899. No longer licensed but is being run as a 'living museum'.
SOURCE	Altyre Burn

℃ 01309-676548
Apr-Sept, 09.30-18.30, last admission at 18.00.
Sun: 14.00-18.30. Oct-Mar, 09.30-16.30, last
admission at 16.00. Sun: 14.00-18.30. Closed
Thu PM and Fri.

VISITORS PER ANNUM	12,000

AGE WHEN BOTTLED	24 years
STRENGTH	59.9%

TASTING NOTES

NOSE	Really rich and full, interwoven with oak smoke, sweetness and malt.
TASTE	Rich, full, clinging and malty with every element in harmony. Finishes most beautifully with haunting traces of oak.
COMMENTS	The entire distillery is run by Historic Scotland and is well worth a visit. An after-dinner treat for all palates from the Rare Malts Selection of United Distillers. A splash of water is essential.

HIGHLAND
SINGLE MALT *SCOTCH WHISKY*

DUFFTOWN

distillery was established near Dufftown at the end of the 19th*. The bright flash of the* KINGFISHER *can often be seen over the DULLAN RIVER, which flows past the old stone buildings of the distillery on its way north to the SPEY. This single HIGHLAND MALT WHISKY is typically SPEYSIDE in character with a delicate, fragrant, almost flowery aroma and taste which lingers on the palate.*

43% vol   AGED **15** YEARS   70 cl

BRAND	**Dufftown**
DISTILLERY	Dufftown
	Dufftown, KEITH, Banffshire AB55 4BR
	01340-820224 01340-820060
MANAGER	Steve McGingle
OWNING COMPANY	United Distillers
PRODUCTION STATUS	Operational
ESTABLISHED	1896
SOURCE	Jock's Well in the Conval Hills
	3 3

AGE WHEN BOTTLED	15 years
STRENGTH	43%

TASTING NOTES	
NOSE	Light, flowery, pleasant aroma.
TASTE	A good, round, smooth taste which tends to linger on the palate.
COMMENTS	Pre-dinner.

BRAND	**Glen Elgin**
DISTILLERY	Glen Elgin
	📠 Longmorn, ELGIN, Morayshire IV30 3SL
	📞 01343-860212 📠 01343-862077
MANAGER	Harry Fox
OWNING COMPANY	United Distillers
PRODUCTION STATUS	Operational
ESTABLISHED	1898-1900
SOURCE	Local springs near Milbuies loch
	🛢 4 🛢 3

AGE WHEN BOTTLED	12 years
STRENGTH	43%

TASTING NOTES	
NOSE	Agreeable aroma of heather and honey.
TASTE	Medium-weight touch of sweetness which finished smoothly.
COMMENTS	The best of both worlds, an excellent all-round malt, suitable for drinking at any time.

BRAND	**Glen Grant**
DISTILLERY	Glen Grant
	ROTHES, Morayshire AB38 7BS
	01542-783300 01542-783306
MANAGER	Willie Mearns
OWNING COMPANY	The Seagram Co Ltd
PRODUCTION STATUS	Operational
ESTABLISHED	1840
SOURCE	The Caperdonich Well
	4 4

01542-783318 01542-783306
Mid-March to Nov, Mon-Fri: 10.00-16.00. Mid-June to mid-Sept, Sat: 10.00-16.00. Sun: 12.30-16.00

OTHER ATTRACTIONS	The Glen Grant Gardens and the Dramming Hut!
VISITORS PER ANNUM	21,000

AGE WHEN BOTTLED	UK market: none given. Export market: 5 years
STRENGTH	40%

TASTING NOTES

NOSE	Light, dry aroma.
TASTE	Dry flavour, light — another good all-round malt.
COMMENTS	Pre-dinner. Hugely popular in Italy.

BRAND	**Glen Keith**
DISTILLERY	Glen Keith
	✉ KEITH, Banffshire AB55 3BU
	☎ 01542-783044 📠 01542-783056
MANAGER	Norman Green
OWNING COMPANY	The Seagram Co Ltd
PRODUCTION STATUS	Operational
ESTABLISHED	1957-60
SOURCE	Balloch Hill springs
	🥃 3 🥃 3

	☎ 01542-783044 📠 01542-783056
	By appointment only

AGE WHEN BOTTLED	10 years
STRENGTH	43%

TASTING NOTES

NOSE	Good, medium aroma with a light aromatic sweetness with a hint of oak.
TASTE	Gentle, dry aromatic fruitiness with a subtle length of warmth and fruit.
COMMENTS	A 'Heritage Selection' malt from Chivas, now repackaged.

BRAND	**Glen Moray**
DISTILLERY	Glen Moray
	ELGIN, Morayshire IV30 1YE
	01343-542577 01343-546195
MANAGER	Edwin Dodson
OWNING COMPANY	Macdonald Martin Distilleries Plc
PRODUCTION STATUS	Operational
ESTABLISHED	1897
SOURCE	River Lossie
	Ex-bourbon
	2 2

Visitors are welcome.
Phone in advance

AGE WHEN BOTTLED	12, 15 years
STRENGTH	40%
SPECIAL BOTTLINGS	1966 (26-y.o.), 1967 (25-y.o.). All at 43%
EXPORT BOTTLINGS	17 years, 43%

TASTING NOTES	12-year-old, 40%
NOSE	Fresh, light aroma
TASTE	Light, pleasant and malty with a clean finish. A fine all-round malt.
COMMENTS	A pre-dinner dram. The 15-year-old is beautifully presented in a regimental tin representing the Queen's Own Cameron Highlanders.

BRAND   **Glen Spey**

DISTILLERY Glen Spey

            ROTHES, Morayshire AB38 7AY

            01340-831215   01340-831356

MANAGER   R. Murray

OWNING COMPANY International Distillers & Vintners Ltd

PRODUCTION STATUS Operational

ESTABLISHED c1878

SOURCE   The Doonie Burn

            2   2

AGE WHEN BOTTLED   8 years

STRENGTH   40%

TASTING NOTES

NOSE   Light, fragrant and delicate.

TASTE   Very smooth and fragrant. A good all-round
            drink.

COMMENTS   Pre-dinner drinking.

BRAND	**Glenallachie**
DISTILLERY	Glenallachie
	ABERLOUR, Banffshire AB38 9LR
	01340-871315/710 01340-871711
MANAGER	Robert Hay
OWNING COMPANY	Campbell Distillers Ltd
PRODUCTION STATUS	Operational
ESTABLISHED	1967-8
SOURCE	Springs on Ben Rinnes
	2 2

AGE WHEN BOTTLED	12 years
STRENGTH	43%

TASTING NOTES

NOSE	Very elegant with a delightful bouquet.
TASTE	Smooth-bodied with a lovely, light, sweet finish. Extremely well-balanced.
COMMENTS	Built by W. Delmé-Evans for Charles Mackinlay & Co Ltd, this distillery produced one of the most underrated malts in Speyside. Now very rare. Only the previous owner's bottling (label shown) may be available from Gordon & Macphail.

MALT	**Glenburgie**
DISTILLERY	Glenburgie-Glenlivet
	▣ FORRES, Morayshire IV36 OQU
	☎ 01343-850258 🖷 01343-850480
MANAGER	Brian Thomas
OWNING COMPANY	Allied Distillers Ltd
PRODUCTION STATUS	Operational
ESTABLISHED	1810
SOURCE	Local springs
	🛢 Mainly ex-bourbon barrels
	⚗ 2 ⚗ 2
OTHER ATTRACTIONS	A very attractively landscaped location
VISITORS PER ANNUM	100

TASTING NOTES	1968, 40%
NOSE	A fragrant, herbal aroma.
TASTE	A light, delicate, aromatic flavour with a pleasant finish.
COMMENTS	A good pre-dinner malt, but only from the independent bottlers. See page 154.

BRAND	**The Glendronach**
DISTILLERY	Glendronach
	Forgue, HUNTLY
	Aberdeenshire AB54 6DB
	01466-730202 01466-730202
MANAGER	Frank Massie
OWNING COMPANY	Allied Distillers Ltd
PRODUCTION STATUS	Operational
ESTABLISHED	1826
SOURCE	Local springs
	European oak, seasoned or ex-sherry
	2 2
	Floor maltings

	01466-730202 01466-730313
	Shop open during office hours. Tours at 10.00 or 14.00.
OTHER ATTRACTIONS	The floor maltings, Highland cattle, 1935 Sentinel steam wagon and the traditional coal-fired stills
AWARDS RECEIVED	'Highly Recommended' by *Decanter Magazine*, 1993
VISITORS PER ANNUM	4000

AGE WHEN BOTTLED	12 years
STRENGTH	40%
EXPORT BOTTLINGS	43% (except Canada)

TASTING NOTES	12-year-old, 40% (The Original)
NOSE	Smooth aroma with a light trace of sweetness.
TASTE	Well-balanced, lingering on the palate with a delicious, long aftertaste.
COMMENTS	A good dram, after-dinner and much sought after.

BRAND	**Glendullan**
DISTILLERY	Glendullan
	📠 Dufftown, KEITH, Banffshire AB55 4DJ
	☎ 01340-820250 🖨 01340-820064
MANAGER	Steve McGingle
OWNING COMPANY	United Distillers
PRODUCTION STATUS	Operational
ESTABLISHED	1897-8
SOURCE	Springs in the Conval Hills
	🍶 3 🍶 3

AGE WHEN BOTTLED	12 years
STRENGTH	43%

TASTING NOTES	
NOSE	Attractive, fruity bouquet.
TASTE	Firm, mellow with a delightful finish and a smooth lingering aftertaste.
COMMENTS	A good after-dinner malt.

PRODUCT OF SCOTLAND

Glenfarclas

10 YEARS OLD
SINGLE HIGHLAND MALT
SCOTCH WHISKY

70cl ℮   40% vol

BRAND	**Glenfarclas**
DISTILLERY	Glenfarclas
	Marypark, BALLINDALLOCH
	Banffshire AB37 9BD
	01807-500209 01807-500234
MANAGER	Mr J. Miller
OWNING COMPANY	J & G Grant
PRODUCTION STATUS	Operational
ESTABLISHED	1836
SOURCE	Springs on Ben Rinnes
	3 3

01807-500257   01807-500234
Mon-Fri: 09.00-16.30 all year.
Sat: 10.00-16 00, June-Sept.

AGE WHEN BOTTLED	8, 10, 12, 15, 21 & 25 years
STRENGTH	40%, 60% for '105'

TASTING NOTES	15-year-old, 46%
NOSE	A rich, delicious promise.
TASTE	Full of character and flavour. One of the great Highland malts.
COMMENTS	Wonderful, fulfilling drinking from a great Speyside distillery.

BRAND	**Glenfiddich**
DISTILLERY	Glenfiddich
	Dufftown, KEITH, Banffshire AB55 4DH
	01340-820373 01340-820805
MANAGER	Bill White
OWNING COMPANY	Wm Grant & Sons Ltd
PRODUCTION STATUS	Operational
ESTABLISHED	1886-7
SOURCE	The Robbie Dubh springs
	Ex-bourbon & sherry
	10 18

01340-820373 01340-820805
Easter to mid-Oct, Mon-Sat: 09.30-16.30.
Sunday: 12.00-16.30. Mid-Oct to Easter, Mon-
Fri: 09.30-16.30.Closed Xmas/New Year.
Groups of more than 12, please phone in
advance. PR Manager: Elizabeth Lafferty

OTHER ATTRACTIONS	Picnic area. AV is in six languages.
VISITORS PER ANNUM	120,000

AGE WHEN BOTTLED	8 years minimum
STRENGTH	40%
EXPORT BOTTLINGS	43%

TASTING NOTES	
NOSE	A light, delicate touch of peat.
TASTE	Attractive flavour, with an after-sweetness. Well-balanced. A good introductory malt.
COMMENTS	If you have never tasted a malt, start with this one. You will not be disappointed.

MALT	**Glenglassaugh**
DISTILLERY	Glenglassaugh
	⌨ PORTSOY, Banffshire AB45 2SQ
	☎ 01261-842367
OWNING COMPANY	The Highland Distilleries Co plc
PRODUCTION STATUS	Mothballed 1986
ESTABLISHED	1875
SOURCE	The Glassaugh Spring

AGE WHEN BOTTLED	12 years
STRENGTH	40%
EXPORT BOTTLINGS	43%

TASTING NOTES	
NOSE	Light, fresh and delicate.
TASTE	Charming, a hint of sweetness which is full of promise with a delicious stimulating follow-through.
COMMENTS	For drinking at any time, but only available from the independent bottlers. See page 154.

BRAND	**The Glenlivet**
DISTILLERY	Glenlivet
	BALLINDALLOCH, Banffshire AB37 9DB
	01542-783220 01542-783220
MANAGER	Jim Cryle
OWNING COMPANY	The Seagram Co Ltd
PRODUCTION STATUS	Operational
ESTABLISHED	1824
SOURCE	Josie's Well
	4 4

	01542-783220 01542-783220
	Easter to end of Oct, Mon-Sat: 10.00-16.00. Sat: 10.00-16.00, July and Aug. Mid-June to mid-Sept: 12.30-16.00.
OTHER ATTRACTIONS	Coffee shop and salad bar.
AWARDS RECEIVED	1995 IWSC: Best Single Malt Scotch Whisky Trophy for malts over 12 years old (18-year old)
VISITORS PER ANNUM	75,000

AGE WHEN BOTTLED	12 & 21 years
STRENGTH	40%, 21-y.o.: 43%
SPECIAL BOTTLINGS	18 years
EXPORT BOTTLINGS	43%

TASTING NOTES	12-year-old, 40%
NOSE	A light, delicate nose with lots of fruit.
TASTE	Medium-light trace of sweetness, quite full on the palate — a first-class malt.
COMMENTS	This one never disappoints. Popular and available everywhere, however, only 1000 bottles of the award-winning 18-year old are available in the UK.

SINGLE MALT *SCOTCH WHISKY*

The three *spirit* stills at the

GLENLOSSIE

distillery have purifiers installed between the lyne arm and the condenser. This has a bearing on the character of the single MALT SCOTCH WHISKY produced which has a fresh, grassy aroma and a smooth, lingering flavour. Built in 1876 by John Duff, the distillery lies four miles south of ELGIN in Morayshire.

A G E D **10** Y E A R S

43% vol   70 cl

BRAND	**Glenlossie**
DISTILLERY	Glenlossie
	ELGIN, Morayshire IV30 3SS
	01343-860331 01343-860302
MANAGER	Dod Winton
OWNING COMPANY	United Distillers
PRODUCTION STATUS	Operational
ESTABLISHED	1876
SOURCE	The Bardon Burn
	3 3

AGE WHEN BOTTLED	10 years
STRENGTH	43%

TASTING NOTES	
NOSE	A soft touch of sweetness with sandalwood overtones.
TASTE	A long-lasting smoothness with an almond-like finish.
COMMENTS	An after-dinner dram from a remote location near Elgin.

THE GLENROTHES DISTILLERY
SAMPLE ROOM

43% vol. 700ml

CHARACTER Fragrant, sherry overtones
CHECKED J.L. Stevens DATE 4/7/84
APPROVED R.H. Frusk DATE 2-11-94
Distilled and Bottled in Scotland. Berry Bros. & Rudd Ltd, 3 St James's Street, London
PRODUCT OF SCOTLAND

DISTILLED IN
1984
BOTTLED IN 1995

SCOTCH WHISKY

BRAND	**The Glenrothes**
DISTILLERY	Glenrothes
	ROTHES, Morayshire AB38 7AA
	01340-831248 01340-831484
MANAGER	A.B. Lawtie
OWNING COMPANY	The Highland Distilleries Co plc
PRODUCTION STATUS	Operational
ESTABLISHED	1878
SOURCE	Local springs
	5 5

AGE WHEN BOTTLED	11 years
STRENGTH	43%

TASTING NOTES	
NOSE	A rich, subtle fragrance of sherry with a light hint of smoke.
TASTE	Excellent balance of soft fruit and malt with an exquisite length of flavour and a smooth, long-lasting finish.
COMMENTS	A limited release of vintage Glenrothes from Berry Bros & Rudd, distilled in 1984.

MALT	**Glentauchers**
DISTILLERY	Glentauchers
	✉ Mulben, KEITH, Banffshire AB55 23L
	☎ 01542-860272 🖨 01542-860327
MANAGER	W.G. Wright
OWNING COMPANY	Allied Distillers Ltd
PRODUCTION STATUS	Operational
ESTABLISHED	1898
SOURCE	Local springs
	🛢 Ex-bourbon
	🝳 3 🝳 3
VISITORS PER ANNUM	25

TASTING NOTES	1979, 40%
NOSE	Light, sweet aroma.
TASTE	Lightly flavoured with a light, dry finish.
COMMENTS	A pre-dinner dram from another distillery founded at the end of the 19th-century. See page 155.

MALT	**Imperial**
DISTILLERY	Imperial
	🖵 Carron, ABERLOUR
	Morayshire AB38 7QP
	☎ 01340-810276 📠 01340-810563
MANAGER	R.S. MacDonald
OWNING COMPANY	Allied Distillers Ltd
PRODUCTION STATUS	Operational
ESTABLISHED	1897
SOURCE	The Ballintomb Burn
	🛢 Ex-bourbon
	⚗ 2 ⚗ 2

- -

TASTING NOTES	1979, 40%
NOSE	Delightful — rich and smoky.
TASTE	Rich and mellow with an absolutely delicious finish. A malt of real character.
COMMENTS	One of the great under-rated malts with a name crying out to be branded. Try it after-dinner. See page 155.

BRAND	**Inchgower**
DISTILLERY	Inchgower
	BUCKIE, Banffshire AB56 2AB
	01542-831161 01542-834531
MANAGER	Douglas Cameron
OWNING COMPANY	United Distillers
PRODUCTION STATUS	Operational
ESTABLISHED	1871
SOURCE	Springs in the Menduff Hills
	2 2

AGE WHEN BOTTLED	14 years
STRENGTH	43%

TASTING NOTES	
NOSE	Very distinctive with a pleasant hint of sweetness.
TASTE	Good, distinctive flavour finishing with a light sweetness.
COMMENTS	A well-balanced malt. After-dinner.

MALT	**Kininvie**
DISTILLERY	Kininvie
	Dufftown, KEITH, Banffshire AB55 4DH
	01340-820373 01340-820805
MANAGER	Bill White
OWNING COMPANY	Wm Grant & Sons Ltd
PRODUCTION STATUS	Operational
ESTABLISHED	1990
SOURCE	The Robbie Dubh springs
	2 6

TASTING NOTES	Not available

BRAND	**Knockando**
DISTILLERY	Knockando
	Knockando, ABERLOUR
	Morayshire AB38 7RD
	☎ 01340-810205 📠 01340-810369
MANAGER	Innes Shaw
OWNING COMPANY	International Distillers & Vintners Ltd
PRODUCTION STATUS	Operational
ESTABLISHED	1898
SOURCE	Cardnach spring
	🜊 2 🜊 2

☎ 0171-258-5000

By appointment only

AGE WHEN BOTTLED	15 years
STRENGTH	40%

TASTING NOTES	
NOSE	Full, pleasant aroma of hot butter.
TASTE	Medium-bodied with a pleasant syrupy flavour which finishes quite quickly.
COMMENTS	After-dinner. Bottled when it is considered ready, rather than at a pre-determined age. The label carries dates of distillation and bottling, currently 1980 and 1995 respectively.

SPEYSIDE
SINGLE MALT
SCOTCH WHISKY

LINKWOOD

distillery stands on the River Lossie,
close to ELGIN in Speyside. The distillery
has retained its traditional atmosphere
since its establishment in 1821.
Great care has always
been taken to safeguard the
character of the whisky which has
remained the same through the
years. Linkwood is one of the
FINEST Single Malt Scotch Whiskies
available - full bodied with a hint of
sweetness and a slightly smoky aroma.

YEARS **12** OLD

43% vol   **70cl**

BRAND	**Linkwood**
DISTILLERY	Linkwood
	☎ ELGIN, Morayshire IV30 3RD
	☎ 01343-547004 📠 01343-549449
MANAGER	Harry Fox
OWNING COMPANY	United Distillers
PRODUCTION STATUS	Operational
ESTABLISHED	c1824
SOURCE	Springs near Milbuies Loch
	🥃 3 🥃 3

By appointment only.

AGE WHEN BOTTLED	12 years
STRENGTH	43%

TASTING NOTES

NOSE	Slightly smoky with a trace of sweetness.
TASTE	Full-bodied hint of sweetness.
COMMENTS	One of the best malts available. Don't pass this one by.

BRAND	**Longmorn**
DISTILLERY	Longmorn
	▣ ELGIN, Morayshire IV30 3SJ
	☎ 01542-783400 🖶 01542-783404
MANAGER	Bob McPherson
OWNING COMPANY	The Seagram Co Ltd
PRODUCTION STATUS	Operational
ESTABLISHED	1894-5
SOURCE	Local springs
	🝊 4 🝊 4
AWARDS RECEIVED	1994 IWSC: Gold Medal

AGE WHEN BOTTLED	15 years
STRENGTH	43%

TASTING NOTES	
NOSE	A delicious, full, fragrant bouquet of spirit.
TASTE	Full bodied, fleshy, nutty and surprisingly refined.
COMMENTS	An oustanding after-dinner dram from the Chivas 'Heritage Selection'.

PRODUCE OF SCOTLAND

ESTABLISHED 1824

The

MACALLAN.

Single Highland Malt

Scotch Whisky

DISTILLED IN

1977

DISTILLED AND BOTTLED BY
THE MACALLAN DISTILLERS LTD.
CRAIGELLACHIE · SCOTLAND
SOLE U.S.A. DISTRIBUTOR
REMY AMERIQUE INC. NEW YORK, N.Y.
ALC/VOL 43% BOTTLED IN SCOTLAND 750ml
BOTTLED IN 1995

BRAND	**The Macallan**
DISTILLERY	Macallan
	Craigellachie, ABERLOUR
	Banffshire AB38 9RX
	01340-871471 01340-871212
MANAGER	Frank Newlands
OWNING COMPANY	The Macallan Distillers PLC
PRODUCTION STATUS	Operational
ESTABLISHED	c1824
SOURCE	Borehole aquifers
	Ex-sherry Spanish oak
	7 14

	01340-871471 01340-871212
	By appointment only. Mon-Fri: tours at 10.00, 11.00, 14.00 & 15.00
OTHER ATTRACTIONS	The location!
AWARDS RECEIVED	Queen's Award for Exports (twice). Architectural awards for HQ building.
VISITORS PER ANNUM	10,000

AGE WHEN BOTTLED	UK: 10, 18 (1976 & 1977 distillations) & 25 years. Export: 7, 12, 18 & 25 years. Italy: 7 years
STRENGTH	7 & 10-y.o: 40%; 12, 18 & 25-y.o: 43%.
EXPORT BOTTLINGS	7, 12 ,18 & 21 years

TASTING NOTES	10-year-old, 40%
NOSE	Smooth, sherry aroma with a silky bouquet.
TASTE	Full-bodied, sherried with a long-lasting aftertaste.
COMMENTS	Still a great masterpiece with an enviable and deserved reputation.

BRAND	**Mannochmore**
DISTILLERY	Mannochmore
	ELGIN, Morayshire IV30 3SS
	01343-860331 01343-860302
MANAGER	Dod Winton
OWNING COMPANY	United Distillers
PRODUCTION STATUS	Mothballed 1995
ESTABLISHED	1970
SOURCE	The Bardon Burn
	3 3

- -

AGE WHEN BOTTLED	12 years
STRENGTH	43%

- -

TASTING NOTES

NOSE	Fresh, light and aromatic with a dry sweetness and a faint smoky background.
TASTE	Delightful, fresh and stimulating, medium-dry creaminess which is both firm and balanced. Long-lasting sweet, dry finish.
COMMENTS	Another excellent all-round drink.

BRAND	**Miltonduff**
DISTILLERY	Miltonduff-Glenlivet
	ELGIN, Morayshire IV30 3TQ
	01343-547433 01343-548802
MANAGER	Stuart Pirie
OWNING COMPANY	Allied Distillers Ltd
PRODUCTION STATUS	Operational
ESTABLISHED	1824
SOURCE	Local water supply
	Ex-bourbon
	3 3

Tours are conducted Mon-Thu, by appointment.

VISITORS PER ANNUM	500

AGE WHEN BOTTLED	12 years
STRENGTH	40%
EXPORT BOTTLINGS	12 years

TASTING NOTES	
NOSE	Agreeable, fragrant bouquet.
TASTE	Medium bodied with a pleasant, well matured, subtle finish.
COMMENTS	After-dinner. Another malt called Mosstowie used to be produced from Lomond-type stills at Miltonduff and is available from the independent bottlers. See page 155.

SPEYSIDE
SINGLE MALT
SCOTCH WHISKY

MORTLACH

was the first of seven
distilleries in *Dufftown*. In the
(19*th farm animals* kept in
adjoining byres were fed on
barley left over from processing
Today water from springs in
the *CONVAL HILLS* is used to
produce this delightful
smooth, fruity single
MALT SCOTCH WHISKY.

A G E D **16** Y E A R S

Distilled & Bottled in SCOTLAND.
MORTLACH DISTILLERY
Dufftown, Keith, Banffshire, Scotland

43% vol   70 cl

BRAND	**Mortlach**
DISTILLERY	Mortlach
	📧 Dufftown, KEITH, Banffshire AB55 4AQ
	☎ 01340-820318 🖷 01340-820018
MANAGER	Ian Millar
OWNING COMPANY	United Distillers
PRODUCTION STATUS	Operational
ESTABLISHED	c1823
SOURCE	Springs in the Conval Hills
	🌢 3 🌢 3

Sales of whisky from distillery office

AGE WHEN BOTTLED	16 years
STRENGTH	43%

TASTING NOTES

NOSE	Full, pleasant, well-rounded aroma with a touch of smoke. Refreshing.
TASTE	Rich and full with a hint of smoke and a pronounced sweetness which imparts a long, full, smooth, sherried finish.
COMMENTS	A first-class after-dinner malt.

Pittyvaich

BRAND	**Pittyvaich**
DISTILLERY	Pittyvaich
	Dufftown, KEITH, Banffshire AB55 4BR
	01340-820561/773
MANAGER	Steve McGingle
OWNING COMPANY	United Distillers
PRODUCTION STATUS	Mothballed 1993
ESTABLISHED	1974
SOURCE	Two major local springs

AGE WHEN BOTTLED	12 years
STRENGTH	43%

TASTING NOTES

NOSE	Rather elegant with a delicate fragrance.
TASTE	Mellow and soft with a fulfilling roundness.
COMMENTS	A remarkably good addition to the bottled malts. An after dinner dram.

BRAND	**The Singleton of Auchroisk**
DISTILLERY	Auchroisk
	🖃 MULBEN, Banffshire AB55 3XS
	☎ 01542-860333 🖶 01542-860265
MANAGER	Graeme Skinner
OWNING COMPANY	International Distillers & Vintners Ltd
PRODUCTION STATUS	Operational
ESTABLISHED	1974
SOURCE	Dorie's Well
	🛢 Predominantly ex-sherry
	🍶 4 🛢 4

By appointment only.

AGE WHEN BOTTLED	10 years minimum, 12 for Japan
STRENGTH	40%
EXPORT BOTTLINGS	43%

TASTING NOTES	1983, 40%
NOSE	Distinctive, attractive bouquet with a touch of fruit.
TASTE	Medium-weight, hint of sweetness with a delicious long-lasting flavour.
COMMENTS	After-dinner. A first class malt international award-winning malt. The Singleton 'Particular' is available only in Japan.

BRAND	**Speyburn**
DISTILLERY	Speyburn
	ROTHES, Morayshire IV33 7AG
	01340-831213 01340-831678
MANAGER	Graham MacWilliam
OWNING COMPANY	Speyburn-Glenlivet Distillery Co., Ltd.
PRODUCTION STATUS	Operational
ESTABLISHED	1897
SOURCE	The Granty Burn sourced on the western slope of the Glen of Rothes.

AGE WHEN BOTTLED	10 years
STRENGTH	40%

TASTING NOTES	
NOSE	A heather-honey bouquet with overtones of peat.
TASTE	Big, full-bodied malty taste with a sweet, lingering finish.
COMMENTS	After-dinner and now widely available under its new owners.

"STRATHISLA"
PURE HIGHLAND MALT
SCOTCH WHISKY
THE OLDEST DISTILLERY IN THE HIGHLANDS
AGED **12** YEARS

BRAND	**Strathisla**
	(Strath-eyela)
DISTILLERY	Strathisla
	KEITH, Banffshire AB55 3BS
	01542-783049 01542-783055
MANAGER	Norman Green
OWNING COMPANY	The Seagram Co Ltd
PRODUCTION STATUS	Operational
ESTABLISHED	1786
SOURCE	Fons Bulliens's Well
	2 2

01542-783044   01542-783039

Just opened and the flagship for the Chivas and Glenlivet Group. Mid-Jan to mid-Dec, Mon-Fri: 09.30-16.30. Sat: 09.30-06.00, July and August. £2 admission charge redeemable in the shop. Under 18s free. Children under the age of 8 cannot enter production area.

OTHER ATTRACTIONS	Free coffee and shortbread, visitor handbook. Nosings.

AGE WHEN BOTTLED	12 years
STRENGTH	43%

TASTING NOTES

NOSE	Beautiful, bewitching fragrance of fruit which also reflects the taste to come.
TASTE	Slender hint of light sweetness with an extremely long, lingering fullness. Good balance.
COMMENTS	An excellent after-dinner malt and one of the best to sip and savour. A Chivas 'Heritage Selection' malt.

BRAND	**Tamdhu**
	(Tamm-doo)
DISTILLERY	Tamdhu
	🖃 Knockando, ABERLOUR
	Morayshire AB38 7RP
	☏ 01340-810221 📠 01340-810255
MANAGER	Dr W. Crilly
OWNING COMPANY	The Highland Distilleries Co plc
PRODUCTION STATUS	Operational
ESTABLISHED	1896-7
SOURCE	A spring beneath the distillery
	🝆 3 🝆 3
	🏛 Saladin maltings

AGE WHEN BOTTLED	10 & 15 years
STRENGTH	40%; 15-year old: 43%

TASTING NOTES	10-year-old, 40%
NOSE	Light aroma with a trace of sweetness.
TASTE	Medium, with a little sweetness and a very mellow finish.
COMMENTS	A good after-dinner dram which is both popular and readily available.

BRAND	**Tamnavulin**
	(Tamna-voolin)
DISTILLERY	Tamnavulin
	🖼 BALLINDALLOCH, Banffshire AB37 9JA
	☎ 01807-590285
OWNING COMPANY	The Whyte & Mackay Group PLC
PRODUCTION STATUS	Non-operational
ESTABLISHED	1965-6
SOURCE	Underground reservoir fed by springs
	🛢 American white oak
	🛢 3 🛢 3

AGE WHEN BOTTLED	10 years
STRENGTH	40%
SPECIAL BOTTLINGS	Stillman's Dram: 25 years
EXPORT BOTTLINGS	43%

TASTING NOTES	10-year-old, 40%
NOSE	Well-matured with a distinct mellowness and a hint of sweetness.
TASTE	Medium weight with a light, smoky, pronounced finish.
COMMENTS	A good all-round malt.

BRAND	**Tomintoul**
	(Tommin-towl)
DISTILLERY	Tomintoul
	BALLINDALLOCH, Banffshire AB37 9AQ
	01807-590274 01807-590342
MANAGER	Mr R. Fleming
OWNING COMPANY	The Whyte & Mackay Group PLC
PRODUCTION STATUS	Operational
ESTABLISHED	1964-5
SOURCE	The Ballantruan Spring
	American white oak, oloroso sherry butts
	2 2

AGE WHEN BOTTLED	8, 12 years
STRENGTH	40%
EXPORT BOTTLINGS	43%

TASTING NOTES	12-year-old, 43%
NOSE	Light and delicate.
TASTE	Light body with good character.
COMMENTS	A good introduction to malt.

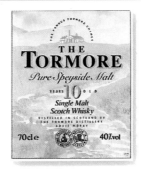

BRAND	**The Tormore**
DISTILLERY	Tormore
	Advie, GRANTOWN-ON-SPEY
	Morayshire PH26 3LR
	01807-510244 01807-510352
MANAGER	John Black
OWNING COMPANY	Allied Distillers Ltd
PRODUCTION STATUS	Operational
ESTABLISHED	1958-60
SOURCE	The Achvochkie Burn
	4 4

By appointment only.
Telephone in advance.

AGE WHEN BOTTLED	10 years
STRENGTH	40%
EXPORT BOTTLINGS	43%

TASTING NOTES	
NOSE	Well-defined dry aroma.
TASTE	Medium-bodied with a hint of sweetness and a pleasant, lingering aftertaste.
COMMENTS	After-dinner.

The Highlands

Outwith the Speyside area distilling activity is spread more sparsely throughout a wide area which I continue to split into four main regions in the North, South, East and West. Although over 30 malts emanate from these four areas, seven are from distilleries no longer in existence. These are Glen Mhor, Glen Albyn and Millburn in Inverness, Banff, Glenugie near Peterhead, Glenury-Royal in Stonehaven and North Port in Brechin. Some other distilleries are closed with only vestiges of them still remaining; these will never open again. These include Coleburn near Elgin, Glenlochy in Fort William, Brora in the town of that name and Glenesk in Montrose. Details on these and other malts are in the chapter Lost Distilleries on page 133.

In the far-flung producing localities around the Highlands the importance of the visitor is often keenly felt and despite the travel required to reach these facilities, Highland hospitality still abounds. The existing distilleries in the Northern region stretch from Dalwhinnie and Speyside near Kingussie to Pulteney at Wick in the north of Caithness and encompass Tomatin at the hamlet of the same name; Royal Brackla near Nairn; Ord Distillery at Muir of Ord in the Black Isle; Dalmore and Teaninich at Alness; Balblair and Glenmorangie near Tain and Clynelish near Brora.

The Eastern malts lie between the Speyside region and the North Sea coast. Banff, the fishing town on the Moray Firth now only possesses one distillery, Glen Deveron. Sadly Glen Garioch Distillery at Oldmeldrum in Aberdeenshire has just been mothballed but will be reinstated when market conditions are more favourable. Royal Lochnagar caters extremely well for the enthusiast with some 35,000 visitors taking advantage not only of its reception centre, but also the proximity to Balmoral Castle each year. To the south-east of Royal Deeside Fettercairn extends the activity to Montrose which used to boast a considerable amount of distilling, but the Glenesk Distillery, (once known as North Esk and also as Hillside) will not produce again and Lochside Distillery (a converted brewery) which once produced both grain and malt whisky, is currently non-operational. I

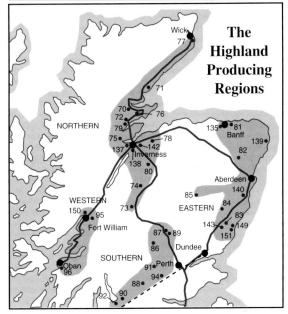

The Highland Producing Regions

Wick 77
71
70
72 76
NORTHERN 135 81
79 Banff
75 78 139
137 142 82
Inverness
138 80 Aberdeen
74 140
85 84
WESTERN 73 EASTERN 83
150 143 149
95 151
Fort William
87 89
86 Dundee
SOUTHERN 91 Perth
Oban 94
96 88
92 90

DISTILLERY LOCATION NUMBERS REFER TO PAGE NUMBERS

have just tasted a dram of Lochside and have listed this in the Lost
Distilleries section on page 133; an independent bottling is also
sometimes available. Further inland, but still on the South Esk river,
Brechin has one producing distillery at Glencadam and a defunct one
at North Port — both of them quite rare malts. South of this arable
region the hills of Perthshire signal the southern limits of the
Highland distilling area.

At Pitlochry the enthusiast can experience two contrasting distilleries. Edradour is the smallest in Scotland and yet maintains all the
advantages of a small 19th-century plant, while Blair Athol is a large,
relatively modern distillery. Aberfeldy Distillery lies at the eastern
entrance to the town of the same name on the banks of the River Tay
and Glenturret Distillery at Crieff lies in a very picturesque location.
Tullibardine at Blackford is a 'recent' distillery (1948) in a village which
not only produces bottled mineral water (Highland Spring) but also has
the only commercial malting floors in Scotland built on arguably the
oldest brewery site in Scotland! And if that amount of diversity is a surprise, Deanston Distillery on the River Teith at Doune, near Stirling,
is a converted cotton mill where the vaulted weaving sheds act as

bonded warehouses and a small hydro-electric generating station is also situated within the plant itself. A gin distillery has also just been brought on stream here!

In the far west of this most southerly of the Highland regions lie Loch Lomond and Glengoyne distilleries. Both almost straddle the Highland line (as does Tullibardine) but claim allegiance to the Highland region. Loch Lomond, built in 1968, produces both Inchmurrin and Old Rhosdhu malts from stills which can facilitate this curious diversity of operation. The owning company has recently taken over Glen Scotia in Campbeltown and Littlemill at Bowling. Glengoyne has a longer pedigree and, resting in a cleft of the Campsie Fells, is a unique distillery in a unique setting.

The Western malts, although only three in number, have suffered only one loss. Glenlochy in Fort William will never produce again, but Oban's distillery, situated just off the High Street of this thriving tourist town, is extremely accessible for the visitor and is one of United Distillers' Classic Malts branded selection. Ben Nevis Distillery in Fort William is also prospering under its Japanese owners and over the last year entertained thousands with the story of 'The Dew of Ben Nevis'!

NORTHERN HIGHLANDS

BRAND	**Balblair**
DISTILLERY	Balblair
	Edderton, TAIN, Ross-shire IV19 1LB
	01862-821273 01862-821360
MANAGER	James Yeats
OWNING COMPANY	Allied Distillers Ltd
PRODUCTION STATUS	Operational
ESTABLISHED	1790
SOURCE	Struie Hill
	2
VISITORS PER ANNUM	800

AGE WHEN BOTTLED	5, 10 years
STRENGTH	40%

TASTING NOTES	10-year-old
NOSE	Pronounced and distinctive fragrance of smoke and sweetness.
TASTE	Good lingering flavour, long-lasting with a slender hint of sweetness.
COMMENTS	A fine dram any time. Bottled by Ballantines.

HIGHLAND
SINGLE MALT
SCOTCH WHISKY

One of the most northerly in Scotland.

CLYNELISH

distillery, was established in *Brora*
by the *Marquess of STAFFORD*
in *1819*. Its building signalled the
end of *illicit distilling*
in the area and provided a
ready market for locally grown
barley. Water is piped from the
CLYNEMILTON burn to produce this
fruity, & slightly smoky single
MALT SCOTCH WHISKY much
appreciated by connoisseurs.

YEARS **14** OLD

43% vol   **70cl**

BRAND	**Clynelish**
	(Kline-leesh)
DISTILLERY	Clynelish
	BRORA, Sutherland KW9 6LR
	01408-621444 01408-621131
MANAGER	Bob Robertson
OWNING COMPANY	United Distillers
PRODUCTION STATUS	Operational
ESTABLISHED	1819, new distillery built 1967
SOURCE	Clynemilton Burn
	6 6

  01408-621444   01408-621131

Mar-Oct, Mon-Fri: 09.30-16.00. Nov-Feb, by appointment only

AWARDS RECEIVED	Gold Award for Safety (ROSPA)
VISITORS PER ANNUM	12,000

AGE WHEN BOTTLED	14 years
STRENGTH	43%

TASTING NOTES

NOSE	Quite peaty for a Northern malt.
TASTE	Rich, pleasant with a slightly dry finish – lots of character.
COMMENTS	Good after-dinner malt. Popular amongst the connoisseurs.

BRAND	**The Dalmore**
DISTILLERY	Dalmore
	☐ ALNESS, Ross-shire IV17 0UT
	☎ 01349-882362 🖶 01349-883655
MANAGER	Mr S. Tulewicz
OWNING COMPANY	The Whyte & Mackay Group PLC
PRODUCTION STATUS	Operational
ESTABLISHED	c1839
SOURCE	Gildermory loch
	🛢 American white oak, oloroso sherry butts
	🛢 4 🛢 4

AGE WHEN BOTTLED	12 years
STRENGTH	40%
SPECIAL BOTTLINGS	Stillman's Dram, 26-year-old
EXPORT BOTTLINGS	43%

TASTING NOTES	
NOSE	Rich, fresh, with a suggestion of sweetness.
TASTE	Full flavour which finishes a touch dry.
COMMENTS	Another really good malt. After-dinner.

BRAND	**Dalwhinnie**
DISTILLERY	Dalwhinnie
	DALWHINNIE, Inverness-shire PH19 1AB
	01528-522240 01528-522240
MANAGER	Robert Christine
OWNING COMPANY	United Distillers
PRODUCTION STATUS	Operational
ESTABLISHED	1897-8
SOURCE	Allt an t'Sluie Burn

01528-522240

Easter-Oct, Mon-Fri: 09.30-16.30.

Other times, by appointment only

VISITORS PER ANNUM	40,000

AGE WHEN BOTTLED	15 years
STRENGTH	43%

TASTING NOTES	
NOSE	A gentle, aromatic bouquet.
TASTE	A luscious flavour with a light honey sweet finish.
COMMENTS	Pre-dinner, and part of United Distillers' Classic Malt range.

BRAND	**Drumguish**
	(Drum-yewish)
DISTILLERY	Speyside
	Tromie Mills, KINGUSSIE
	Inverness-shire PH21 1NS
	01540-661060 01540-661959
MANAGER	Richard Beattie
OWNING COMPANY	Speyside Distillery Co Ltd
PRODUCTION STATUS	Operational
ESTABLISHED	1990
SOURCE	River Tromie
OTHER ATTRACTIONS	Borders a wildlife sanctuary

AGE WHEN BOTTLED	No age given
STRENGTH	40%

TASTING NOTES

NOSE	Pleasant, malty aroma with a delicate hint of sweetness and apple blossom.
TASTE	Very smooth, delicate sweetness importing fruitiness to the palate. Well-balanced with a lingering, gentle finish.
COMMENTS	A welcome addition to Scotland's malt portfolio.

BRAND	**Glen Ord**
DISTILLERY	Glen Ord
	MUIR OF ORD, Ross-shire IV6 7UJ
	01463-870421 01463-870101
MANAGER	Kenny Gray
OWNING COMPANY	United Distillers
PRODUCTION STATUS	Operational
ESTABLISHED	1838
SOURCE	Lochs Nan Eun and Nam Bonnach
	3 3

	01463-871334 01463-870101
	Mon-Fri: 09.30-16.30
OTHER ATTRACTIONS	ASVA commended exhibition
AWARDS RECEIVED	IWSC, House of Campbell Trophy for best single malt up to 15 years old. Grand Gold Medal at the Monde Selection.
VISITORS PER ANNUM	25,000

AGE WHEN BOTTLED	12 years
STRENGTH	40%

TASTING NOTES	
NOSE	A beautifully deep nose, with a tinge of dryness.
TASTE	Good depth with a long-lasting, delicious aftertaste. Very smooth.
COMMENTS	After-dinner, readily available and winning awards!

BRAND	**Glenmorangie**
DISTILLERY	Glenmorangie
	🖃 TAIN, Ross-shire IV19 1PZ
	☎ 01862-892043 🖷 01862-893862
MANAGER	Dr Bill Lumsden
OWNING COMPANY	Macdonald Martin Distilleries plc
PRODUCTION STATUS	Operational
ESTABLISHED	1843
SOURCE	Tarlogie Springs
	🛢 Ex-bourbon
	🛢 4 🛢 4

🕉 🎥 🍷 ☎ 01862-892477
🚻R 🕆 Visitors are welcome. Phone in advance.

AGE WHEN BOTTLED	10, 18 years
STRENGTH	40%, 43% and cask strength
SPECIAL BOTTLINGS	'Port Wood'

TASTING NOTES	10-year-old, 40%
NOSE	Beautiful aroma. Fresh and sweet with a subtle hint of peat.
TASTE	Medium-bodied with a sweet, fresh finish. One to linger and dwell upon.
COMMENTS	An excellent malt, very popular. Entire distillery output is sold as single, bottled malt.

MALT	**Pulteney**
	(Pult-nay)
DISTILLERY	Pulteney
	Huddart Street, WICK
	Caithness KW1 5BA
	01955-602371 01955-602279
MANAGER	Donald Reitt
OWNING COMPANY	Inverhouse Distillers Ltd
PRODUCTION STATUS	Operational
ESTABLISHED	1826
SOURCE	Mains water

TASTING NOTES	8-year-old, 40%
NOSE	Fine, delicate, light aroma with a hint of the island malts.
TASTE	Light, crisp and refreshing with a hint of fullness which gives a positive, lengthy finish.
COMMENTS	An excellent aperitif whisky from the most northerly mainland distillery which has just changed hands. A branded bottling may be made available in the future. Also available as Old Pulteney from the independent bottlers. See page 155.

BRAND	**Royal Brackla**
DISTILLERY	Royal Brackla
	Cawdor, NAIRN, Nairnshire IV12 5QY
	01667-404280 01667-404743
MANAGER	Chris Anderson
OWNING COMPANY	United Distillers
PRODUCTION STATUS	Operational
ESTABLISHED	c1812
SOURCE	The Cawdor Burn
	2 2

AGE WHEN BOTTLED	10 years
STRENGTH	43%

TASTING NOTES

NOSE — Refreshing aroma of peat smoke with a delicate hint of sweetness and a floral overtone.

TASTE — Round, medium-sweet with a fullness which becomes dry on the palate but then has a lingering, tender sweetness which is almost sherry-like.

COMMENTS — Excellent and refreshing. This distillery was the first to receive the Royal prefix which was given by William IV. A new label and a new persona for a fine malt.

The *County Firth* is one of the few places in the British Isles inhabited by *PORPOISE*. They can be seen quite regularly, swimming close to the shore ... less than a mile from

TEANINICH

distillery founded in 1817 in the *Ross-shire* town of *ALNESS*, the *distillery* is now one of the largest in *Scotland*. *TEANINICH* is an *assertive single MALT WHISKY* with a *spicy, smoky, satisfying* taste.

A G E D **10** Y E A R S

43% vol   70cl

BRAND	**Teaninch**
DISTILLERY	Teaninich
	ALNESS, Ross-shire IV17 0XB
	01349-882461 01349-883864
MANAGER	Angus Paul
OWNING COMPANY	United Distillers
PRODUCTION STATUS	Operational
ESTABLISHED	1817
SOURCE	The Dairywell Spring
	3 3

AGE WHEN BOTTLED	10 years
STRENGTH	43%

TASTING NOTES	
NOSE	Fresh, light touch of smoke with a hint of fruit and a delicate sweetness.
TASTE	Medium balance with a gentle oakiness and a smooth, long finish.
COMMENTS	An excellent all-rounder.

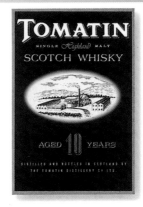

BRAND	**Tomatin**
DISTILLERY	Tomatin
	🖃 TOMATIN, Inverness-shire IV13 7YT
	☎ 01808-511444 📠 01808-511373
MANAGER	T.R. McCulloch
OWNING COMPANY	Subsidiary of Takara Shuzo & Okura & Co Ltd
PRODUCTION STATUS	Operational
ESTABLISHED	1897
SOURCE	Allt na Frithe Burn
	🌡 12 🌡 11

☎ 01808-511444   📠 01808-511373
Mon-Fri: 09.00-16.30 (last tour at 16.30). Sat,
May-Oct: 09.30-13.00 (last tour at 12.00). Book
in advance for large parties during Dec/Jan.

VISITORS PER ANNUM	70,000

AGE WHEN BOTTLED	10 years
STRENGTH	40%
SPECIAL BOTTLINGS	Limited edition — 25-year old
EXPORT BOTTLINGS	10 & 12 years, 40 & 43%

TASTING NOTES	10-year-old
NOSE	Pleasant and light.
TASTE	Light body, very smooth.
COMMENTS	A pre-dinner dram and a good introduction to malt whisky. The distillery was the first to be acquired by the Japanese in 1985 and is one of Scotland's largest.

EASTERN HIGHLANDS

BRAND	**Glen Deveron**
DISTILLERY	Macduff
	BANFF, Banffshire AB4 3JT
	01261-812612 01261-818083
MANAGER	Michael Roy
OWNING COMPANY	Bacardi Ltd
PRODUCTION STATUS	Operational
ESTABLISHED	1960
SOURCE	Local spring
	2 3
AWARDS RECEIVED	1993/4 IWSC: Silver medal

AGE WHEN BOTTLED	12 years
STRENGTH	40%
EXPORT BOTTLINGS	5 & 12 years, 43%

TASTING NOTES

NOSE	Assertive, refreshing bouquet.
TASTE	Medium-weight and a smooth, pleasant flavour with a clean finish.
COMMENTS	An after-dinner dram which is also available as Macduff from the independent bottlers. See page 155.

See page 155.

BRAND	**Glen Garioch**
	(Glengeerie)
DISTILLERY	Glen Garioch
	Oldmeldrum, INVERURIE
	Aberdeenshire AB51 0ES
	01651-872706 01651-872578
MANAGER	Ian Fyfe
OWNING COMPANY	Morrison Bowmore Distillers Ltd, now part of Suntory
PRODUCTION STATUS	Mothballed 1995
ESTABLISHED	1798
SOURCE	Springs on Percock Hill
	Ex-bourbon & sherry
	2 2
	Floor maltings

AGE WHEN BOTTLED	1984, 12, 15 & 21 years
STRENGTH	1984, 12 y.o: 40%; 15, 21 y.o: 43%
EXPORT BOTTLINGS	1984; 12, 15 & 21-y.o.

TASTING NOTES	21-year-old
NOSE	Delicate and smoky.
TASTE	Pronounced, peaty flavour with a smooth, pleasant finish.
COMMENTS	A good after-dinner dram.

MALT	**Glencadam**
DISTILLERY	Glencadam
	☞ BRECHIN, Angus DD9 7PA
	☎ 01356-622217 📠 01356-624926
MANAGER	G. Harper
OWNING COMPANY	Allied Distillers Ltd
PRODUCTION STATUS	Operational
ESTABLISHED	c1825
SOURCE	Loch Lee

♿	☎ 01356-624212
	Mon-Thu: afternoon tours.
OTHER ATTRACTIONS	Nature trail, public park.
VISITORS PER ANNUM	400

TASTING NOTES	1974, 40%
NOSE	Light hint of sweetness.
TASTE	Full, with quite a fruity flavour and a good finish.
COMMENTS	An after-dinner malt. See page 154.

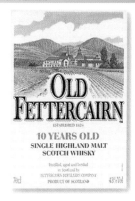

BRAND	**Old Fettercairn**
DISTILLERY	Fettercairn
	📧 Distillery Road, LAURENCEKIRK
	Kincardineshire AB30 1YE
	📞 01561-340244 📠 01561-340447
MANAGER	Mr B. Kenny
OWNING COMPANY	The Whyte & Mackay Group PLC
PRODUCTION STATUS	Operational
ESTABLISHED	c1824
SOURCE	Springs in the Grampian Mountains
	🛢 American white oak, oloroso sherry butts
	⚗ 2 ⚗ 2

	📞 01561-340205
	Open May to Sept, Mon-Sat: 10.00-16.30 (last
	tour at 16.00)
VISITORS PER ANNUM	10,000

AGE WHEN BOTTLED	10 years
STRENGTH	40%
EXPORT BOTTLINGS	43%

TASTING NOTES	
NOSE	Light, stimulating fresh aroma.
TASTE	Fresh, slightly dry finish which is quite
	stimulating but gently restrained.
COMMENTS	A good all-round drink. Reputed to be the
	second distillery licensed after the legislation of
	1823.

BRAND	**Royal Lochnagar**
DISTILLERY	Royal Lochnagar
	Crathie, BALLATER
	Aberdeenshire AB35 5TB
	01339-742273 01339-742312
MANAGER	Alastair Skakles
OWNING COMPANY	United Distillers
PRODUCTION STATUS	Operational
ESTABLISHED	1845
SOURCE	Local springs below Lochnagar

	01339-742273 01339-742312
	Easter-October, Mon-Sun: 10.00-17.00.
	November-Easter: Mon-Fri, 10.00-17.00.
OTHER ATTRACTIONS	Balmoral Castle is close by.
AWARDS RECEIVED	Loo of the Year Award!
VISITORS PER ANNUM	35,000

AGE WHEN BOTTLED	12 years and no age given
STRENGTH	40% and 43%

TASTING NOTES	12-year-old, 40%
NOSE	Pleasant, full nose.
TASTE	Good body with a full, malt-fruit-like taste and a delicious trace of sweetness.
COMMENTS	Royal Lochnagar Selected Reserve is a special bottling available from time to time at 43%. Expect to pay around £159!

SOUTHERN HIGHLANDS

HIGHLAND
SINGLE MALT
SCOTCH WHISKY

ABERFELDY

distillery was established in
1898 on the *road* to *Perth* and
south side of the *RIVER TAY.*
Fresh *spring* water is taken
from the nearby *PITILIE*
burn and used to produce this
UNIQUE single MALT
SCOTCH WHISKY with its
distinctive PEATY nose.

A G E D **15** Y E A R S

43% vol 70cl

BRAND	**Aberfeldy**
DISTILLERY	Aberfeldy
	✉ ABERFELDY, Perthshire PH15 2EB
	☎ 01887-820330 📠 01887-829432
MANAGER	Brian Bissett
OWNING COMPANY	United Distillers
PRODUCTION STATUS	Operational
ESTABLISHED	1896
SOURCE	Pitilie Burn
	⚱ 2 ⚱ 2

  ☎ 01887-820330   📠 01887-820432

Easter–Oct, Mon–Fri: 10.00–16.00. Restricted
opening times in winter

OTHER ATTRACTIONS	Nature trail
VISITORS PER ANNUM	10,000

AGE WHEN BOTTLED	15 years
STRENGTH	43%

TASTING NOTES	
NOSE	Fresh clean with a lightly peated nose.
TASTE	Substantial flavour with a good round taste.
COMMENTS	Now rising in popularity as a UD brand.

BRAND	**Blair Athol**
DISTILLERY	Blair Athol
	▣ PITLOCHRY, Perthshire PH16 5LY
	☎ 01796-472161 📠 01796-473292
MANAGER	Gordon Donoghue
OWNING COMPANY	United Distillers
PRODUCTION STATUS	Operational
ESTABLISHED	1798
SOURCE	Allt Dour
	🛢 2 🛢 2

	☎ 01796-472234 📠 01796-473292
	Easter-Sept, Mon-Sat: 09.00-17.00. Sun: 12.00-17.00. Oct-Easter, Mon-Fri: 09.00-17.00 (last tour at 16.00). Dec-Feb, tours by appointment only
OTHER ATTRACTIONS	Coffee shop
VISITORS PER ANNUM	50,000

AGE WHEN BOTTLED	12 years
STRENGTH	43%

TASTING NOTES	
NOSE	Light, fresh, clean aroma.
TASTE	Medium hint of peat with a round finish. Plenty of flavour.
COMMENTS	A fine south-Perthshire malt suitable for pre-dinner drinking.

BRAND	**Deanston**
DISTILLERY	Deanston
	🖃 DOUNE, Perthshire FK16 6AG
	☎ 01786-841422 🖷 01786-841439
MANAGER	Ian Macmillan
OWNING COMPANY	Burn Stewart Distillers plc
PRODUCTION STATUS	Operational
ESTABLISHED	1965-6, from the cotton mill established on same site c1785
SOURCE	River Teith
	🛢 American & Spanish oak hogsheads & butts, some fresh sherry butts
	🝪 2 🝪 2

AGE WHEN BOTTLED	12 years, 17 & 21 for export
STRENGTH	40%

TASTING NOTES	12-year-old
NOSE	Fresh, light hint of sweetness with a slightly dry, nasal effect and a hint of malt.
TASTE	Medium sweetness, light, smooth with an attractive long smooth finish.
COMMENTS	A very refreshing and stimulating dram from a distillery sited beside a fine salmon river.

BRAND **The Edradour**

(Edra-dower)

DISTILLERY Edradour

PITLOCHRY, Perthshire PH16 5JP

01796-473524 01796-472002

MANAGER John Reid

OWNING COMPANY Campbell Distillers Ltd

PRODUCTION STATUS Operational

ESTABLISHED 1837

SOURCE Local springs on Mhoulin Moor

01796-472095 01796-472002

Mon-Sat: 09.30-17.00. Sun: 12.00-17.00

VISITORS PER ANNUM 100,000

AGE WHEN BOTTLED 10 years

STRENGTH 40%

EXPORT BOTTLINGS 43%

TASTING NOTES

NOSE Fruity-sweet and smoky.

TASTE Light marzipan taste which comes through smooth, slightly dry and malty with a nutty almond-like aftertaste.

COMMENTS Scotland's smallest distillery and therefore closest to a working 19th-century distillery. Well worth a visit to see how it used to be done.

BRAND	**Glengoyne**
DISTILLERY	Glengoyne
	📧 DUMGOYNE, Stirlingshire G63 9LB
	☎ 01360-550229 📠 01360-550094
MANAGER	Ian Taylor
OWNING COMPANY	Lang Brothers Ltd
PRODUCTION STATUS	Operational
ESTABLISHED	c1833
SOURCE	Distillery Burn from Campsie Hills
	🛢 Refill whisky & ex-sherry oak
	🛢 🛢 2

☎ 01360-550254 📠 01360-550094

Hourly tours, Mon-Sat: 10.00-16.00 (last tour at 16.00). Sun: 12.00-16.00 (last tour at 16.00)

OTHER ATTRACTIONS	Specially booked dinners can be arranged
AWARDS RECEIVED	Recommended by the Scottish Tourist Board
VISITORS PER ANNUM	40,000

AGE WHEN BOTTLED	10, 12 & 17 years.
STRENGTH	10 y.o: 40%; 17 y.o: 43%
SPECIAL BOTTLINGS	Vintage bottlings distilled on Christmas Day, 1967
EXPORT BOTTLINGS	12 years, 40 & 43%

TASTING NOTES	10-year-old
NOSE	A light, fresh aroma.
TASTE	Light, pleasant, well-balanced and moreish.
COMMENTS	Another great introduction to malts. The 17-year old is impressive. Only unpeated malt is used at Glengoyne.

BRAND	**The Glenturret**
DISTILLERY	Glenturret
	The Hosh, CRIEFF, Perthshire PH7 4HA
	01764-656565 01764-654366
MANAGER	George Cameron
OWNING COMPANY	The Highland Distilleries Co plc
PRODUCTION STATUS	Operational
ESTABLISHED	1775
SOURCE	Loch Turret
	Refill whisky, ex-bourbon & sherry

	01764-656565 01764-654366
	Heritage Centre with Water of Life, Spirit of the Glen Exhibition & Pagoda Room. Mar-Dec, Mon-Sat: 09.30-16.30. Jan-Feb, Mon-Fri: 11.30-14.30. Tourist manager: Philippa Ireland.
OTHER ATTRACTIONS	Smuggler's Restaurant
AWARDS RECEIVED	1974, 1981 & 1991 IWSC: Gold Medal.
VISITORS PER ANNUM	215,414

AGE WHEN BOTTLED	12, 15, 18 years
STRENGTH	40%
SPECIAL BOTTLINGS	1966, 24-y.o, 40%; 15-y.o, 50%; 25-y.o Decanter, 40%; 21-y.o Flagon, 40%; Malt Liqueur, 35%
EXPORT BOTTLINGS	12 years & Malt Liqueur

TASTING NOTES	12-year-old
NOSE	Very impressive aromatic nose.
TASTE	Full, lush body with a good depth of flavour and a stimulating finish. Delightful.
COMMENTS	Scotland's oldest distillery.

BRAND	**Inchmurrin**
DISTILLERY	Loch Lomond
	ALEXANDRIA, Dunbartonshire G83 0TL
	01389-752781 01389-757977
MANAGER	J. Peterson
OWNING COMPANY	Loch Lomond Distillery Co Ltd
PRODUCTION STATUS	Operational
ESTABLISHED	1966
SOURCE	Loch Lomond
	2 2

AGE WHEN BOTTLED	10 years
STRENGTH	40%

TASTING NOTES	
NOSE	Slightly aromatic. Follows through on the palate.
TASTE	Light-bodied. Most of the flavour is on the front of the palate and thus finishes quickly.
COMMENTS	An everyday drinking malt.

BRAND	**Old Rhosdhu**
DISTILLERY	Loch Lomond
	ALEXANDRIA, Dunbartonshire G83 0TL
	01389-752781 01389-757977
MANAGER	J. Peterson
OWNING COMPANY	Loch Lomond Distillery Co Ltd
PRODUCTION STATUS	Operational
ESTABLISHED	1966
SOURCE	Loch Lomond
	2 2

AGE WHEN BOTTLED	5 years
STRENGTH	40%

TASTING NOTES

NOSE	Aromatic, rich, malty and sweet
TASTE	Light-bodied, sweet and clean. Most of the flavour and taste is on the front of the palate and finishes quite quickly.
COMMENTS	An dram for drinking at any time.

PRODUCT of SCOTLAND

Tullibardine

SINGLE HIGHLAND MALT
SCOTCH WHISKY

*A Single Malt Scotch Whisky of quality
and distinction distilled and bottled by*
TULLIBARDINE DISTILLERY LIMITED
BLACKFORD   PERTHSHIRE   SCOTLAND

40%vol   70cl

BRAND	**Tullibardine**
	(Tully-bardeen)
DISTILLERY	Tullibardine
	Blackford, AUCHTERARDER
	Perthshire PH4 1QG
	01764-682252
OWNING COMPANY	The Whyte & Mackay Group PLC
PRODUCTION STATUS	Non-operational
ESTABLISHED	1949
SOURCE	The Ochil Hills
	American white oak
	2 2

AGE WHEN BOTTLED	10 years
STRENGTH	40%
SPECIAL BOTTLINGS	25-year old Stillman's Dram occasionally available.
EXPORT BOTTLINGS	43%

TASTING NOTES	
NOSE	Delicate, mellow, sweet aroma of fruit.
TASTE	Full bodied, with a fruity flavour and a good lingering finish.
COMMENTS	A pre-dinner dram from another distillery designed by W. Delmé-Evans.

WESTERN HIGHLANDS

BRAND	**Ben Nevis**
DISTILLERY	Ben Nevis
	🖃 FORT WILLIAM, Inverness-shire PH33 6TJ
	☎ 01397-702476 📠 01397-702768
MANAGER	A.W. (Colin) Ross
OWNING COMPANY	Ben Nevis Distillery (Fort William) Ltd
PRODUCTION STATUS	Operational
ESTABLISHED	c1825
SOURCE	Allt a Mhullin on Ben Nevis
	🛢 Remade bourbon hogsheads & fresh ex-sherry butts
	🛢 2 🛢 2

🏠 🎥 📺 ♿R ♨	☎ 01397-700200
	Jan-Oct: 09.00-17.00
OTHER ATTRACTIONS	Snack bar
AWARDS RECEIVED	ASVA commended
VISITORS PER ANNUM	40,000

AGE WHEN BOTTLED	26 years
STRENGTH	Cask strength

TASTING NOTES	26-year-old, 54.6%
NOSE	Sweet, malty bouquet. Very distinctive.
TASTE	Dances on the palate with a full-bodied firmness. Light, aromatic with a delicious length of flavour.
COMMENTS	With a minute dash of water, this is an exceedingly fine after-dinner drink. Highly recommended. Bottling strengths will vary from cask to cask.

43% vol — 70 cl e

BRAND	**Oban**
DISTILLERY	Oban
	✉ Stafford Street, OBAN, Argyll PA34 5NH
	☎ 01631-562110 📠 01631-563344
MANAGER	Ian Williams
OWNING COMPANY	United Distillers
PRODUCTION STATUS	Operational
ESTABLISHED	c1794
SOURCE	Loch Gleann a' Bhearraidh

☎ 01631-564262   📠 01631-563344

Open all year. Mon-Fri: 09.30-17.00 also Saturday from Easter to October. Last tour at 16.15.

AWARDS RECEIVED	ASVA commended
VISITORS PER ANNUM	35,000

AGE WHEN BOTTLED	14 years
STRENGTH	43%

TASTING NOTES

NOSE	Fresh hint of peat.
TASTE	Firm, malty flavour finishing very smoothly. Quite silky.
COMMENTS	One of United Distillers' Classic Malt range. An excellent any time dram.

The Lowlands

The modern difference between Lowland malt and that originating from the other regions is simply one of style. Historically, the distinguishing factors were more numerous. In the late 18th century the product of the discreet Highland still (be it legal or illegal) was considered a wholesome, hand-crafted product which was in great demand in the urban markets, but the larger Lowland distillers produced a relatively coarse whisky (rarely made purely from malted barley alone) in huge industrial stills in an effort to supply both the city drinkers and the lucrative London market. This distinction was created by the industrial Lowland distillers who aggressively exploited whatever Government legislation was in force. The distinctions were magnified by the drawing of the 'Highland Line' which effectively stretched from Greenock on the Clyde to Dundee on the Tay and split the country into two regions 'gauged' by two separate sets of Excise regulations due to the disparity between their respective products.

Eventually the technical differences were removed when more realistic early 19th-century Government Acts encouraged illicit distillers in the Highlands to go legal and allowed all producers to distil on a more equal basis. With the recent closures of the Caledonian, Carsebridge, Garnheath and Cambus grain distilleries, there is less to remind us of the days when the Steins and the Haigs wielded some of the most powerful industrial might in Scotland. In those days, the grain distillers were enormously important to the economy of the central belt.

Similarly, Lowland malt distilleries were once in abundance even in the late 19th century. In the remote south-west corner over a dozen concerns existed stretching from Stranraer to Annan. Only Bladnoch Distillery survives and is unlikely ever to produce again; a sad loss when one considers some of the great vintage whiskies this charming distillery has produced. The remains of two distilleries at Langholm (Glen Tarras and Langholm) and Annan (Annandale) can still be viewed but they are now merely reminders of a bygone age.

Most of the Lowland malts are now produced to the north along the Highland line. In the Glasgow area, just north of the Clyde along the A82 route to Loch Lomond lies Auchentoshan Distillery, which is

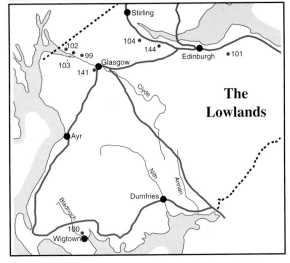

DISTILLERY LOCATION NUMBERS REFER TO PAGE NUMBERS

the only remaining Lowland distillery still employing the technique of triple-distillation. The nearby Littlemill Distillery at Bowling employed triple distillation until the 1930s but is currently closed. Kinclaith malt still exists although the distillery is now no longer in existence having once been part of Long John's Strathclyde grain distilling complex. Another malt in a similar position is Inverleven which emanates from the curious 'Lomond' stills at the malt distillery within Allied Distillers' vast grain distillery at Dumbarton.

The other Lowland triple-distilled malt used to be produced at Rosebank, near Falkirk. This is one of the great Lowland malts, highly regarded as a pre-dinner dram and a wonderful surprise to anyone drinking their first malt whisky. That Rosebank has been mothballed is immensely sad and it is to be hoped that this fine malt will one day run from the stills again. St Magdalene at Linlithgow did not escape this fate and is now defunct but the malt is still available as one of United Distiller's Rare Malts Selection.

Much of Edinburgh's prosperity has been built on brewing and distilling although the industry is greatly reduced within the city now. There are no malt distilleries operating now and any activity is concentrated in producing grain whisky at North British Distillery. However, to the east of the city Glenkinchie Distillery at Pencaitland was one of the first to cater for visitors. This malt is bottled as a brand under the Classic Malts banner by United Distillers. All the Lowland drams are worth tracking down and are an excellent introduction to malt whisky.

BRAND	**Auchentoshan**
DISTILLERY	Auchentoshan
	DALMUIR, Dunbartonshire G81 4SG
	01389-878561 01389-877368
MANAGER	Stuart Hodkinson
OWNING COMPANY	Morrison Bowmore Distillers Ltd, now part of Suntory
PRODUCTION STATUS	Operational
ESTABLISHED	c1800
SOURCE	Kilpatrick Hills
	Ex-bourbon & sherry
	plus 1 intermediate
AWARDS RECEIVED	1992 IWSC: Gold Medal (21-year-old); 1994, Gold Medal (21-year-old)

AGE WHEN BOTTLED	10, 21 years (1972)
STRENGTH	'Select', 10 y.o: 40%; 21 y.o: 43%
SPECIAL BOTTLINGS	'Select': no age given.
EXPORT BOTTLINGS	'Select'; 10 & 21 y.o.

TASTING NOTES	10-year-old
NOSE	Delicate, slightly sweet.
TASTE	Light, soft sweetness with a good aftertaste.
COMMENTS	A triple-distilled malt which is readily available at home and abroad and winning awards.

BRAND	**Bladnoch**
DISTILLERY	Bladnoch
	✉ BLADNOCH, Wigtownshire DG8 9AB
	☏ 01988-402235
OWNING COMPANY	United Distillers
PRODUCTION STATUS	Mothballed 1993
ESTABLISHED	1817
SOURCE	Loch Ma Berry

AGE WHEN BOTTLED	10 years
STRENGTH	43%

TASTING NOTES	
NOSE	Very light, aromatic and delicate.
TASTE	Smooth, delicate but full and easy to drink.
COMMENTS	Scotland's most southerly distillery. A pre-dinner malt which is exceptional in vintage bottlings.

BRAND	**Glenkinchie**
DISTILLERY	Glenkinchie
	PENTCAITLAND, East Lothian EH34 5ET
	01875-340333 01875-340854
MANAGER	Alastair Robertson
OWNING COMPANY	United Distillers
PRODUCTION STATUS	Operational
ESTABLISHED	c1837
SOURCE	Lammermuir Hills

	01875-340451 01875-340854
	Mon-Fri: 09.30-16.00
OTHER ATTRACTIONS	Museum of distilling with many artefacts.
VISITORS PER ANNUM	18,000

AGE WHEN BOTTLED	10 years
STRENGTH	43%

TASTING NOTES	
NOSE	Light, fragrant sweetness.
TASTE	Round flavour, slightly dry with a lingering smoothness.
COMMENTS	An excellent pre-dinner dram, and one of United Distillers' Classic Malt range.

MALT	**Inverleven**
DISTILLERY	Inverleven
	📧 DUMBARTON, Dunbartonshire G82 1ND
	📞 01389-765111 📠 01389-723081
OWNING COMPANY	Allied Distillers Ltd
PRODUCTION STATUS	Mothballed 1991
ESTABLISHED	1938
SOURCE	Loch Lomond

TASTING NOTES	17-year-old, 46%
NOSE	Delicate hint of smoke.
TASTE	Quite full-bodied. Smooth with a round palate.
COMMENTS	Rarely available unless obtained from one of the independent bottlers. See page 155.

BRAND	**Littlemill**
DISTILLERY	Littlemill
	BOWLING, Dunbartonshire G60 5BG
	01389-874154
MANAGER	J. Peterson
OWNING COMPANY	Loch Lomond Distillery Co Ltd
PRODUCTION STATUS	Mothballed 1992
ESTABLISHED	1772
SOURCE	Kilpatrick Hills

AGE WHEN BOTTLED	8 years
STRENGTH	40%
EXPORT BOTTLINGS	40 & 43%

TASTING NOTES	
NOSE	Light and delicate.
TASTE	Mellow-flavoured, light, slightly cloying, yet pleasant and warming.
COMMENTS	Pre-dinner, from a distillery full of interesting, novel features. Certainly one of the oldest in Scotland.

LOWLAND
SINGLE MALT
SCOTCH WHISKY

*Established on its present
site at CAMELON in 1840*

ROSEBANK

*distillery stands on the
banks of the FORTH
and CLYDE CANAL.
This was once
a busy thoroughfare with
boats and steamers
continually passing by;
it is still the source
of water for cooling.
This single MALT
SCOTCH WHISKY is
triple distilled which
accounts for its light
distinctive nose and well
balanced flavour.*

A G E D **12** Y E A R S

ROSEBANK DISTILLERY
Falkirk, Stirlingshire, Scotland
43% vol 70cl

BRAND	**Rosebank**
DISTILLERY	Rosebank
	Camelon, FALKIRK, Stirlingshire FK1 5BW
	01324-623325
OWNING COMPANY	United Distillers
PRODUCTION STATUS	Mothballed 1993
ESTABLISHED	c1840
SOURCE	Carron Valley reservoir

AGE WHEN BOTTLED	12 years
STRENGTH	43%

TASTING NOTES	
NOSE	Light and delicate.
TASTE	Well-balanced, good flavour with an acceptable astringency.
COMMENTS	A triple-distilled malt suitable for pre-dinner drinking.

Islay

Of all Scotland's malts, the Islays are perhaps the most characteristic. But even so, there are some surprises within this group which are traditionally held to be amongst the heaviest and most pungent available. Their most recognisable characteristics are due to production methods which were developed in concert with the available distilling ingredients in this remote locality. While the mainland markets were supplied by mainland distillers in the 18th and 19th centuries, the islanders supplied a local market from stills — both legal and illegal — which were operated from farmyards, bothies on the bleak moors above Port Ellen and remote caves along the precipitous coast of the Oa.

Islay, renowned as the most fertile island in the Hebrides, had three major assets in this development, a ready source of local barley — or bere as it was then known — inexhaustible amounts of peat and burns running brim-full of soft water. Coupled to this was the likelihood that the art of distilling was probably brought to Scotland via Islay by the Irish in the 15th century. It is impossible to visit Islay and not notice the peat. Along the roadside crossing the enormous Laggan Moss between Port Ellen and Bowmore the peat banks spread as far as the eye can see. This fuel was the only means by which the islanders could dry their grain which was an essential process not only for distilling, but also for storage during the wet seasons. By kilning barley it could be kept longer and the dryer the grain was, the less likely it was to go mouldy.

As the grain dried in the fumes, the peat imparted to the barley a highly distinctive character which manifested itself when the spirit was finally distilled from it. These characteristics are still apparent in today's Islay malts and are best experienced by trying Ardbeg, Lagavulin and Laphroaig which form the three most traditional Islay malts. The other Islays display this peaty-smoky characteristic to a lesser degree but it is always detectable nonetheless.

It is good to see that the Islay distillers, despite their more remote location, are always able to accommodate visitors and some of the distilleries are spectacularly situated. All of them have one thing in com-

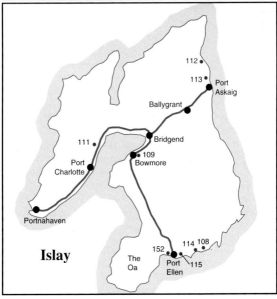

DISTILLERY LOCATION NUMBERS REFER TO PAGE NUMBERS

mon — they are built on the seashore. A century ago this afforded them the access to the sea and thus the mainland markets. The smaller inland farmyard distilleries had by then been unable to compete and, one by one, they closed down. But it is still possible to see the sites of these traditional distilleries, most notably at Octomore Farm behind Port Charlotte, at Tallant Farm above Bowmore and at Lossit Kennels by Bridgend. Of the present distilleries perhaps Bowmore is most favourably endowed for the visitor. Not only does it produce a memorable dram but is has a superb reception centre and in one of its bonded warehouses the Islay and Jura community have built a public swimming pool which is heated by the distillery processes!

In the south of the island Lagavulin and Laphroaig both cater well for the visitor and are magnificently located by the sea. Ardbeg is a more sobering prospect given that the distillery was once the centre of a large community in the 19th century, but at least it is producing which is something that can never again be said about Port Ellen which will never reopen. However, the associated maltings behind the distillery are supplying not only Lagavulin and Caol Ila with malt, but also some of the other non-UD distilleries on the island.

Across Loch Indaal from Bowmore lies Bruichladdich which, like

Bunnahabhain, produces one of the lighter Islays. This distillery was one of the first in the Hebrides to be constructed from concrete in 1881 and is currently mothballed. It is unlikely that its owners will allow it to go the way of Port Ellen since it is such a respected malt with a fine reputation, especially in Italy. Near Port Askaig, at the point where you take the ferry crossing to Jura, lie Caol Ila and Bunnahabhain with spectacular views of the Paps of Jura. Caol Ila is as modern and efficient a distillery as you are likely to find and the stillhouse alone is worth seeing. The dram is now readily available and it is a good Islay, as is its close neighbour which was built in 1880-1.

Bunnahabhain is for many people the best introduction to the Islays since it is neither too heavy nor too light, and for many it remains their favourite Islay dram. The Islays should be approached with great respect since they are considered as essential components by master-blenders who, without them, would be left with a very much reduced palette from which to create the Scotch blends which have been the bedrock of the industry's success the world over.

BRAND	**Ardbeg**
DISTILLERY	Ardbeg
	📧 PORT ELLEN, Islay, Argyll PA42 7DU
	📞 01496-302244
MANAGER	Iain Henderson
OWNING COMPANY	Allied Distillers Ltd
PRODUCTION STATUS	Operational
ESTABLISHED	1815
SOURCE	Lochs Arinambeast and Uigedale
	🛢 American oak barrels

AGE WHEN BOTTLED	10 years
STRENGTH	40%

TASTING NOTES

NOSE	Lovely peaty aroma with a hint of sweetness.
TASTE	Full-bodied and luscious with an excellent aftertaste.
COMMENTS	A filling after-dinner malt. Retains a low profile as a brand, it has a huge following amongst enthusiasts.

BRAND	**Bowmore**
DISTILLERY	Bowmore
	BOWMORE, Islay, Argyll PA43 7JS
	01496-810441 01496-810757
MANAGER	James McEwan
OWNING COMPANY	Morrison Bowmore Distillers Ltd, now part of Suntory
PRODUCTION STATUS	Operational
ESTABLISHED	c1770
SOURCE	River Laggan
	Ex-bourbon & sherry
	2 2
	Floor maltings

01496-810441

The best in the islands. Mon-Fri: 10.00 until last tour at 15.30.

Admission: £2 adults, £1 pensioners.

AWARDS RECEIVED	1992 IWSC: Best Single Malt Trophy, 21-year old. 1994, Best Special Edition Malt, Black Bowmore
VISITORS PER ANNUM	8000

AGE WHEN BOTTLED	10, 12, 15, 17, 21, 22, 25 & 30 years. Legend: no age given.
STRENGTH	Legend, 10: 40%. Black, 49%. All others: 43%.
SPECIAL BOTTLINGS	Duty Free: Surf (no age given) & Mariner, 15-y.o. Final release of 'Black', 1964 in late 1995 with 1812 bottles. 22 & 25-y.o. are ceramics.

EXPORT BOTTLINGS	Legend, 12, 17, 21, 22, 25 & 30-y.o., Black.

TASTING NOTES	10-year-old
NOSE	Light, peaty-smoky.
TASTE	Healthy, middle-range Islay with medium weight and a smooth finish.
COMMENTS	One of the best sherrying malts available — the older vintages are outstanding. The swimming pool in one of the bonds makes Bowmore a unique experience! The company is the 1995 Distiller of the Year.

BRAND	**Bruichladdich**
	(Broo-ich-laddie)
DISTILLERY	Bruichladdich
	BRUICHLADDICH, Islay, Argyll PA49 7UN
	01496-850221
OWNING COMPANY	The Whyte & Mackay Group PLC
PRODUCTION STATUS	Non-operational
ESTABLISHED	1881
SOURCE	Private dam
	2 2

AGE WHEN BOTTLED	10, 15 & 21 years
STRENGTH	40%
SPECIAL BOTTLINGS	Stillman's Dram, currently 26 years
EXPORT BOTTLINGS	10, 15 & 21 y.o., 40 & 43%

TASTING NOTES	10-year-old
NOSE	Light to medium with a good hint of smoke.
TASTE	Lingering flavour giving the expected fullness of Islay character whilst lacking the heavier tones.
COMMENTS	A good pre-dinner dram, which is an ideal introduction to the Islay style. The 15-year-old is superb.

BRAND   **Bunnahabhain**
                      (Bu-na-ha-venn)

DISTILLERY   Bunnahabhain
                      PORT ASKAIG, Islay, Argyll PA46 7RP
                      01496-840646   01496-840248

MANAGER   Mr J.A. Proctor
OWNING COMPANY   The Highland Distilleries Co plc
PRODUCTION STATUS   Operational
ESTABLISHED   1883
SOURCE   Local springs
                      2   2

Visitors are welcome by appointment

VISITORS PER ANNUM   1000

AGE WHEN BOTTLED   12 years
STRENGTH   40%
EXPORT BOTTLINGS   43%

TASTING NOTES
NOSE   Pronounced character with a flowery aroma.
TASTE   Not reminiscent of the Islay style, but a lovely
                     round flavour nonetheless.
COMMENTS   A popular after-dinner dram especially in France
                     and the United States.

ISLAY
SINGLE MALT *SCOTCH WHISKY*

CAOL ILA

distillery, built in 1846 is situated near Port Askaig on the Isle of Islay. Steamers used to call twice a week to collect whisky from this remote site in a cove facing the Isle of Jura. Water supplies for mashing come from Loch nam Ban although the sea provides water for condensing. Unusual for an Islay this single MALT SCOTCH WHISKY has a fresh aroma and a light yet well rounded flavour.

A G E D **15** Y E A R S

43% vol   *Distilled & Bottled in SCOTLAND. CAOL ILA DISTILLERY, Port Askaig, Isle of Islay, Scotland* **70cl**

BRAND	**Caol Ila**
	(Koal-eela)
DISTILLERY	Caol Ila
	PORT ASKAIG, Islay, Argyll PA46 7RL
	01496-840207 01496-840660
MANAGER	Mike Nicolson
OWNING COMPANY	United Distillers
PRODUCTION STATUS	Operational
ESTABLISHED	1846
SOURCE	Loch Nam Ban
	3 3

Visiting by appointment.

OTHER ATTRACTIONS	The views from the stillhouse over to Jura!
VISITORS PER ANNUM	2000

AGE WHEN BOTTLED	15 years
STRENGTH	43%

TASTING NOTES

NOSE	Light, fresh, slightly peated.
TASTE	Medium-bodied with a rounded flavour. Finishes smoothly. Not as heavy as some other Islays.
COMMENTS	Popular after-dinner dram. Sherried bottlings are excellent.

BRAND	**Lagavulin** *(Lagga-voolin)*
DISTILLERY	Lagavulin PORT ELLEN, Islay, Argyll PA42 7DZ 01496-302400 01496-302321
MANAGER	Mike Nicolson
OWNING COMPANY	United Distillers
PRODUCTION STATUS	Operational
ESTABLISHED	1816 with distilling on the site since at least 1784
SOURCE	Solum Lochs 2 2

01496-302250

Visiting by appointment.

OTHER ATTRACTIONS	The ruins of the Macdonald stronghold of Dun Naomhaig *(Dunn-aaveg)* stand nearby.
VISITORS PER ANNUM	2000

AGE WHEN BOTTLED	16 years
STRENGTH	43%

TASTING NOTES

NOSE	Heavy, powerful, peat-smoke aroma. Unmistakable.
TASTE	Robustly full-bodied, well-balanced and smooth with a hint of sweetness on the palate.
COMMENTS	One of United Distillers' Classic Malt range. A remarkable Islay malt and a great way to round off a hearty meal.

LAPHROAIG®

SINGLE ISLAY MALT
SCOTCH WHISKY

10
Years Old

The most richly flavoured of
all Scotch whiskies
ESTABLISHED
1815

DISTILLED AND BOTTLED IN SCOTLAND BY
D. JOHNSTON & CO. (LAPHROAIG), LAPHROAIG DISTILLERY, ISLE OF ISLAY.

40% vol   70 cl

BRAND	**Laphroaig**
	(La-froyg)
DISTILLERY	Laphroaig
	PORT ELLEN, Islay, Argyll PA42 7DU
	01496-302418 01496-302496
MANAGER	Iain Henderson
OWNING COMPANY	Allied Distillers Ltd
PRODUCTION STATUS	Operational
ESTABLISHED	1815
SOURCE	Kilbride Dam
	Ex-Kentucky bourbon
	3 4
	Floor maltings

&R	Visitors area. Telephone in advance. Some items for sale.
AWARDS RECEIVED	By appointment to H.R.H Prince of Wales. Queen's Award for Export Achievement, 1994. IWSC 1993, Gold Medal (10-y.o.)
VISITORS PER ANNUM	3500

AGE WHEN BOTTLED	10, 15 years
STRENGTH	40%
SPECIAL BOTTLINGS	Duty free: 1977 at 43%.
EXPORT BOTTLINGS	43% for export.

TASTING NOTES	10-year-old
NOSE	Unmistakable. Medicinal, well-balanced, peaty-smoky.
TASTE	Full of character, big peaty flavour with a delightful touch of sweetness. Betrays its proximity to sea.
COMMENTS	An excellent after-dinner malt from a beautifully situated distillery. Very popular.

Campbeltown

Dufftown could lay claim to being Scotland's whisky capital but in the middle of the last century there was only one place which had the right to that name — Campbeltown. Situated on the lee shore of the Mull of Kintyre, this town was literally awash with distillate a hundred years ago. When Alfred Barnard compiled his wonderful book — The Whisky Distilleries of the United Kingdom in 1886, he found no less than 21 producing distilleries in and around the town!

These were Hazelburn (established 1836), Springbank (1828), Dalintober (1832), Benmore (1868), Ardlussa (1879), Dalaruan (1824), Lochead (1824), Glen Nevis (1877), Kinloch (1823), Burnside (1825), Glengyle (1873), Lochruan (1835), Albyn (1830), Scotia (1832), Rieclachan (1825), Glenside (1830), Longrow (1824), Kintyre (c1826), Campbeltown(1815), Argyll (1844) and Springside (1830).

The number of operations were a throwback to the days when illic-it distillation in the district was rife, and was not entirely discouraged by the landowners, or indeed by the law. Campbeltown's boom period was based upon a ready and huge market in cheap Scotch within the working population in the industrial central belt and the avaricious desire of the distillers to supply that market come what may.

A local coal seam seemed perfect as a cheap source of fuel, but its exhaustion was to prove fatal, and as the late Victorian boom in whisky distilling collapsed so too did distilling in Campbeltown. The sad reminder of the industry's presence in the town is now manifested in two distilleries, Glen Scotia and Springbank, of which only Springbank is currently producing two styles of whisky.

It would be unwise to forget Campbeltown's contribution to distill-ing despite the fact that it is unlikely more distilleries will ever start up in the town again. Its product had a unique regional flavour which came close to the Islay style. This can still be found in Longrow, a traditional old-fashioned malt which is distilled at Springbank. Its character differs from its sister malt Springbank which is a smoother, more elegant dram. That it has succeeded so well is a tribute to the family which has always owned the distillery and which has always recognised its quality.

When Barnard visited the town he noted that '... Sunday in

Campbeltown is carried to its Jewish length, and is quite a day of gloom and penance... it is said that there are as many places of worship as distilleries in the town'. His remarks, no matter how flippant, are important since they set down a precise record of the 'Golden Age' of distilling in Scotland — a time we are unlikely to experience again. If Campbeltown's decline has served any purpose at all, it will have been to remind us all of the fickle nature of the marketplace.

As a town, Campbeltown is delightfully situated. Its remoteness allows its inhabitants a certain privacy from the mainstream tourist traffic during the summer, but it is always worth considering the detour down the Mull of Kintyre when travelling through this part of the world. The overwhelming impression is that of a thriving fishing and market town, but the names of old distilleries are to be found in a number of nameplaces — Ardlussa, Lochruan, Dalintober and the like. Savour them as you savour a dram in this setting — I have always said that drinking malt at source is the best way to appreciate it. Try it in Campbeltown.

BRAND	**Glen Scotia**
DISTILLERY	Glen Scotia
	12 High Street, CAMPBELTOWN
	Argyll PA28 6DS
	01586-552288
MANAGER	J. Peterson
OWNING COMPANY	Loch Lomond Distillery Co Ltd
PRODUCTION STATUS	Mothballed 1994
ESTABLISHED	1832
SOURCE	Campbeltown Loch

AGE WHEN BOTTLED	14 years
STRENGTH	40%
EXPORT BOTTLINGS	43%

TASTING NOTES	
NOSE	An intense aroma with a touch of smoke. Delicate and sweet.
TASTE	Light for a Campbeltown with a hint of peat and a clean finish.
COMMENTS	A pre-dinner dram. In fact, a good drink at any time.

BRAND	**Longrow**
DISTILLERY	Springbank
	📠 CAMPBELTOWN, Argyll PA28 6ET
	📞 01586-552085 📠 01586-553215
MANAGER	John C.A. McDougall
OWNING COMPANY	J & A Mitchell & Co Ltd
PRODUCTION STATUS	Operational
ESTABLISHED	1824
SOURCE	Crosshill Loch
	🛢 Refill whisky, ex-sherry & bourbon
	🍶 🍶 2
	⛪ Floor maltings

TASTING NOTES	1974, 46%
NOSE	An island-peaty, medicinal aroma.
TASTE	Well balanced, with a hint of sweetness. A succulent malty palate and a fine lingering aftertaste. Almost an Islay.
COMMENTS	Distilled at Springbank, but by using entirely peat-dried malted barley, the heavier peated malt results. A dram for the connoisseur, a 1973 cask of which has just been released. In 1997, a 10-y.o. will be readily available.

BRAND	**Springbank**
DISTILLERY	Springbank
	CAMPBELTOWN, Argyll PA28 6ET
	01586-552085 01586-553215
MANAGER	John C.A. McDougall
OWNING COMPANY	J & A Mitchell & Co Ltd
PRODUCTION STATUS	Operational
ESTABLISHED	1828
SOURCE	Crosshill Loch
	Refill whisky, ex-sherry & bourbon
	2
	Floor maltings

AGE WHEN BOTTLED	15, 21, 25 & 30 years
STRENGTH	46%
SPECIAL BOTTLINGS	5 y.o. available in Martinique bottles in the UK.

TASTING NOTES	21-year-old
NOSE	Positive, rich aroma with a slight sweetness.
TASTE	Well-balanced, full of charm and elegance. A malt drinker's dream.
COMMENTS	A dependable classic for the malt lover and superb after-dinner drink. Bottled at the distillery and now widely available.

The Islands

Archaeological finds a few years ago on the island of Rhum in the Inner Hebrides suggest that the natives knew how to make a brew long before the Irish were credited with introducing the art of distillation to their Scottish cousins. Wm Grant & Sons Ltd (makers of Balvenie, Kininvie and Glenfiddich) even went so far as to try and recreate the original 4000-year-old recipe which was scientifically reconstructed from scrapings off pottery shards. This brew was drawn from the local herbs, grasses and other vegetation and turned out to be a little immature, but like all good brews it improved with familiarity.

The last two centuries may have gradually familiarised the world to Scotch, but we can now lay claim to having played a fundamental part in the history of the development of distillation. And for the present-day visitor to Scotland, the past is manifested in some of the most gloriously situated distilleries in the world.

The most recent addition to the island portfolio is Arran Distillery at Lochranza which has just begun production. We shall have to wait a few years before we can judge the product but it is a positive sign in a tough marketplace that the owners and backers have gone ahead with the development. Visitor facilities will be up to standard so a visit to this stunning island will not be considered complete without a stop at Lochranza to sample the malt.

The styles of the other island malts differ, partly due to location and partly due to the desires of the distillery operators. For instance Jura, from the island just north of Islay, can be fairly described as a Highland-like dram whereas in the last century it was much closer in style to its Islay neighbours. The reason is that the distillery went out of production in 1901 and was replaced in 1963 with a completely new unit designed by the Welsh distillery builder William Delmé-Evans. He had stills of a highland-type design installed and used malt that was only lightly peated. Similarly Tobermory's distillery has had its plant changed over the years and has produced some variable distillations of Ledaig until ceasing production in 1980. Happily, it came back on stream in May 1990 and a recent

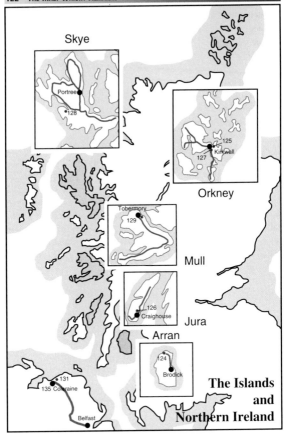

Skye

Portree•
•128

Orkney

125
Kirkwall
127

Tobermory
129

Mull

126
Craighouse

Jura

Arran

124
Brodick

**The Islands
and
Northern Ireland**

•131
135 Coleraine

Belfast

DISTILLERY LOCATION NUMBERS REFER TO PAGE NUMBERS

takeover by Burn Stewart Distillers PLC seems to have secured its foreseeable future.

On Skye an altogether more traditional taste is found. Talisker is one of the giants among malt. It is a 'big' whisky in every way with an explosive effect on the palate and a wonderful, peaty, sweetness on the nose. The distillery has changed considerably but still retains some of the more traditional implements associated with 18th and 19th-century distilling. For instance, swan-necked lyne arms can be seen dropping into wooden worm tubs outside the stillhouse wall — the same technique illicit distillers used in their bothies. Notwithstanding the untested Arran distillate, Talisker's taste is perhaps the most recognisable among the island and western malts and has benefited greatly from being included in the Classic Malts selection from UD.

Orkney is the most northerly outpost of whisky distilling in Scotland with two very good malts emanating from Highland Park and Scapa. The former is operational while the latter has been mothballed since 1993. The only development to offset this decline in activity has been the success of the Orkney Brewery which has recently expanded and is now supplying the mainland with ales with the enchanting names of Dragonhead Stout and Skullsplitter! However, if an independent brewery can be established in such a location and succeed, does this not raise the question as to whether an independent distillery could be run on Orkney? If anyone were to assume that it simply could not be done, then I suggest they look to Arran for my answer. The island distillers were always tough and dedicated and they fought hard to survive. With Arran now on stream and Tobermory back in the fold, we might yet see a resurgence of Hebridean distilling activity as the millennium closes.

BRAND	**Highland Park**
DISTILLERY	Highland Park
	KIRKWALL, Orkney KW15 1SU
	01856-873107 01856-876091
MANAGER	Mr W.J. Morgan
OWNING COMPANY	The Highland Distilleries Co plc
PRODUCTION STATUS	Operational
ESTABLISHED	1798
SOURCE	Cattie Maggie's Spring
	2 2
	Floor maltings

01856-874619   01856-876091

Apr-Oct, Mon-Fri: 10.00-17.00 (last tour 16.00). Jul & Aug, Mon-Fri: 10.00-17.00 plus Sat/Sun: 12.00-17.00. Nov/Dec/Mar, Mon-Fri: Tours at 14.00 & 15.30. Jan/Feb, closed: Tours by appointment only.

OTHER ATTRACTIONS	The traditional floor maltings
VISITORS PER ANNUM	16,000

AGE WHEN BOTTLED	12 years
STRENGTH	40%
SPECIAL BOTTLINGS	1967 vintage at 43%
EXPORT BOTTLINGS	43% in some export countries

TASTING NOTES

NOSE	Full of character — pleasant, lingering and smoky.
TASTE	Medium, well-balanced flavour finishing with a subtle dryness.
COMMENTS	An excellent after-dinner dram from Scotland's most northerly distillery.

BRAND	**Isle of Jura**
DISTILLERY	Isle of Jura
	Craighouse, JURA, Argyll PA60 7XT
	01496-820240 01496-820344
MANAGER	Willie Tait
OWNING COMPANY	The Whyte & Mackay Group PLC
PRODUCTION STATUS	Operational
ESTABLISHED	c1810, rebuilt in 1960-3
SOURCE	Loch A'Bhaile Mhargaidh (or Market Loch)
	American white oak, small proportion of oloroso sherry butts
	2 2

Visitors are welcome by appointment

AGE WHEN BOTTLED	10 years
STRENGTH	40%
SPECIAL BOTTLINGS	Stillman's Dram, currently 26 years
EXPORT BOTTLINGS	43%

TASTING NOTES	10-year-old
NOSE	Dry and tart. Smooth with subtle peaty traces.
TASTE	Well-matured, full but delicate flavour. Good lingering character.
COMMENTS	An almost Highland-like malt created by W. Delmé-Evans for drinking at any time.

MALT	**Scapa**
DISTILLERY	Scapa
	KIRKWALL, Orkney KW15 1SE
	01856-872071 01856-876585
MANAGER	R.S. MacDonald
OWNING COMPANY	Allied Distillers Ltd
PRODUCTION STATUS	Mothballed 1993
ESTABLISHED	1885
SOURCE	Lingro Burn and local springs
	Ex-bourbon barrels

TASTING NOTES	1983, 40%
NOSE	Delightful aromatic bouquet of peat and heather. Slightly rich.
TASTE	Medium-bodied with a malty, silk-like finish. Good, long-lasting flavour.
COMMENTS	After-dinner, but only from the independent bottlers. See page 155. The Navy rescued Scapa from destruction by fire during the First World War!

BRAND	**Talisker**
DISTILLERY	Talisker
	CARBOST, Skye IV47 8SR
	01478-640203 01478-640401
MANAGER	Mike Copland
OWNING COMPANY	United Distillers
PRODUCTION STATUS	Operational
ESTABLISHED	1830-33
SOURCE	Cnoc-nan-Speireag (Hawkhill)
	2 3

	Apr-Oct, Mon-Fri: 09.00-16.30. Jul-Aug, Mon-Sat: 09.00-16.30. Nov-Mar, 14.00-16.30. Large parties advised to book in advance. AV in winter only.
OTHER ATTRACTIONS	Two moorings available for visiting yachts and note the swan-necked stills and the wooden worm tubs outside the stillhouse.
AWARDS RECEIVED	ASVA commended
VISITORS PER ANNUM	40,000

AGE WHEN BOTTLED	10 years
STRENGTH	45.8%

TASTING NOTES	
NOSE	Heavy, sweet and full aroma.
TASTE	Unique full flavour which explodes on the palate, lingering with an element of sweetness.
COMMENTS	Superb after-dinner malt from United Distillers' Classic Malt range. One of the best.

BRAND	**Tobermory**
DISTILLERY	Tobermory
	▤ TOBERMORY, Mull, Argyll PA75 6NR
	☎ 01688-302645 📠 01688-302643
MANAGER	Ian Macmillan. Asst: Alan McConnochie
OWNING COMPANY	Burn Stewart Distillers plc
PRODUCTION STATUS	Operational
ESTABLISHED	1798
SOURCE	Private loch
	🛢 American & Spanish oak hogsheads & butts
	🛢 2 🛢 2

🏭 🎥 🥃 ✉ ☎ 01688-302647   📠 01688-302643

Easter-Sept, Mon-Fri: 10.00-17.00.

VISITORS PER ANNUM	8000

AGE WHEN BOTTLED	No age given
STRENGTH	40%

TASTING NOTES	
NOSE	A light but definite sweetness with soft, gentle overtones.
TASTE	Good, light to medium flavour, softly aromatic, sweet overtones which give good balance. Finishes with a hint of smokiness.
COMMENTS	A most welcome island malt. made from unpeated barley. Also available as Ledaig, 1974 at 43%, made from peated barley. See page 155.

Northern Ireland

Today whiskey-making in the province is solely represented by Bushmills in County Antrim, but it was once more widespread and even today, some remnants of the past can still be savoured in the bottle. If you have a spare £400 or thereabouts, you can buy one of the last remaining bottles of 34-year-old Coleraine single malt whiskey made at the distillery of the same name which ceased production of malt whiskey in 1964.

Whereas Irish whiskey is distilled from a mash containing both malted and unmalted barley, the main difference between Scotch malt and the Irish variety is that the latter is distilled three times as opposed to twice. (Exceptions to this are Springbank and Auchentoshan). This inevitably leads to a spirit with lower fractions of fusel oil and other constituents which help give Scotch malt its more complex character. This in no way detracts from the end-product which is of a high quality when experienced as Bushmills 10-year-old. Their 5-year-old is only available in Italy. Among their other malts waiting to come on the market is their 19-year-old Millennium Malt which you can order now in time for the end of the century.

The distillery caters well for the whiskey enthusiast and is situated on the stunning Antrim coastline overlooking the North Channel to Scotland, which is the very stretch of water over which the secrets of distilling were brought to Scotland many hundreds of years ago. Such a heritage is perhaps more apparent from the fact that the distillery received its first licence to distil on 20 April, 1608 with a tradition of activity on the site stretching even further back to 1276. Notwithstanding the discoveries on Rhum, there can be little doubt that the Scots owe their distilling pedigree to a large degree to their Irish cousins.

At this point it is worth noting that the establishment of another distillery, albeit at Dundalk in the Republic, now means that there is another source of Irish malt whiskey with supplies of The Tyrconnell now finding their way into the UK.

BRAND	**Bushmills**
DISTILLERY	Old Bushmills

BUSHMILLS, Co. Antrim BT57 8XH

01265-731521 01265-731339

MANAGER	Mr Frank McHardy
OWNING COMPANY	Irish Distillers Group Ltd
PRODUCTION STATUS	Operational
ESTABLISHED	1608
SOURCE	St Columb's Rill

Mainly ex-bourbon & sherry

4 5

&R ⌖

01265-731521 01265-731339

Very popular. Advisable to telephone in advance.
Mon-Thu: 09.00-12.00,13.30-16.00. In summer,
Fri: 09.00-16.00. Sat: 10.00-16.00

OTHER ATTRACTIONS	Giant's Causeway and Dunluce Castle are nearby.
AWARDS RECEIVED	Queen's Award for Export Achievement, 1986,
	1991. 1995 IWSC, Gold Medal (10-year-old)
VISITORS PER ANNUM	70,000

AGE WHEN BOTTLED	10 years
STRENGTH	40%
SPECIAL BOTTLINGS	16, 19 years. Duty Free: 10-y.o., 43%
EXPORT BOTTLINGS	5-year-old in Italy. 10-year-old worldwide at
	43%.

TASTING NOTES	10-year-old
NOSE	Warm, sweet bouquet with hints of sherry, vanilla and honey.
TASTE	Smooth and malty due to triple-distillation and traditional absence of peat giving a subtle combination of flavours.
COMMENTS	An after-dinner dram from the oldest licensed whiskey distillery in the world.

Lost Distilleries

The following distilleries are non-operational due to the fact that they are either no longer in existence, or closed and have no prospect of ever reopening. Their product is still available from various sources and labels have been reproduced where the original proprietors have issued the malt as a commercial brand. The first group are distilleries which simply do not exist any more. In some cases a vestige of the original structure remains (such as St Magdalene at Linlithgow), but these malts really have gone forever. The second group are distilleries which still exist, but are only ghost structures which may eventually find alternative uses. They will certainly never re-open again.

The reasons for these closures and shut-downs are almost all the same. The whisky industry has over the last 100 years been subject to a cyclical pattern of supply and demand. In many cases distilleries were owned by companies which found that they had too much bonded stock on hand at times when supply far outstripped demand. In these circumstances many distilleries were shut down in order to conserve stocks and reduce production capacity and overheads. Obviously, the first type of distillery to close in these circumstances was the more remote and less well known one, which would be producing malt solely for the fillings trade and would not have the cachet or reputation of some of the more prominent 'crack' whiskies, which were in great demand from the blenders as constituent parts of their blended brands.

Many of these distilleries also suffered from poor design and lack of convenient access for modern transport. Furthermore, distillery closures often occur when companies merge and the whisky industry has been no stranger to the merging of producing companies into much larger units. Whilst this is of obvious benefit to the export trade, shareholders and the constituent merger partners, it obviously does reduce the whisky heritage throughout Scotland. It would appear that the most recent spate of mothballings and closures has satisfied the cost accountants. One distillery which I am rather pleased to list in this section is Lochside in Montrose. In the past I have had extreme difficulty in trying to get a sample of the product and information regarding the distillery, but I am pleased to say that, due to the kindness of Charlie

Sharpe, the manager there, I have been able to sample the last of the production of this malt and give as much detail on the distillery as possible.

This distillery has been subjected to a recent change in ownership in that it is now part of Allied Distillers, but it is still answering to its former owners based in Spain. This change has come about with the recent merger of Allied and the Domecq sherry group to form Allied Domecq. Unless there is some change in the company philosophy regarding Lochside Distillery, it seems unlikely that it will ever produce again, but there is a faint possibility that this might not happen. If it did produce again it would be a happy ending to a chapter which contains some particularly memorable drams. It is sad that a town such as Inverness, which once boasted three distilleries, the produce of which in some cases was outstanding, now does not have a single distillery to speak of.

DEFUNCT DISTILLERIES

BRAND	**Banff**
DISTILLERY	Banff
	BANFF, Banffshire
PRODUCTION STATUS	Closed 1983. Dismantled
ESTABLISHED	1863

TASTING NOTES	1974, 40%
NOSE	Very light with a trace of smoke.
TASTE	Slightly aggressive, finishing a touch fiery. Nonetheless a good bite.
COMMENTS	A rare dram from a distillery which is now effectively dead. Seek out the vintages while you can. See page 153.

BRAND	**Coleraine**
DISTILLERY	Coleraine
	🖃 COLERAINE, Co. Antrim
PRODUCTION STATUS	Closed 1964. No longer exists
ESTABLISHED	1820

AGE WHEN BOTTLED	34 years
STRENGTH	57.1%

TASTING NOTES	Not available
COMMENTS	Not surprisingly I was unable to taste this dram, which, I assume will be snapped up by collectors since there are very few bottles left. A piece of Ulster distilling history without a doubt.

MALT	**Glen Albyn**
DISTILLERY	Glen Albyn
	INVERNESS, Inverness-shire
PRODUCTION STATUS	Closed 1983. Dismantled 1986
ESTABLISHED	c1846

TASTING NOTES	20-year-old, 46%
NOSE	Light and smoky. Pleasant.
TASTE	Well-rounded, smoky with a full finish.
COMMENTS	See page 154. Now a collector's item.

MALT	**Glen Mhor**
DISTILLERY	Glen Mhor
	INVERNESS, Inverness-shire
PRODUCTION STATUS	Closed 1983. Dismantled 1986
ESTABLISHED	1892

TASTING NOTES	8-year-old, 40%
NOSE	Light, sweet fragrance.
TASTE	Light-bodied with a slightly dry finish.
COMMENTS	Another collector's dram. See page 154.

MALT	**Glenugie**
DISTILLERY	Glenugie
	PETERHEAD, Aberdeenshire
PRODUCTION STATUS	Closed 1983. No longer there
ESTABLISHED	c1831

TASTING NOTES	20-year-old, 46%
NOSE	Hint of ripe fruit.
TASTE	Initial trace of sweetness. Firm, malty but with a quick, dry finish.
COMMENTS	A rare pre-dinner dram, see page 155.

MALT	**Glenury-Royal**
DISTILLERY	Glenury-Royal
	▣ STONEHAVEN, Kincardineshire
OWNING COMPANY	United Distillers
PRODUCTION STATUS	Closed 1985. Will not reopen
ESTABLISHED	c1825
SOURCE	Cowie Water

AGE WHEN BOTTLED	12 years
STRENGTH	40%

TASTING NOTES	
NOSE	A light hint of smoke with a dry aroma.
TASTE	Light body with a dry, smoky finish.
COMMENTS	A good introductory malt, suitable for pre-dinner drinking but currently unavailable.

Established 1842

CADENHEAD'S
AUTHENTIC
COLLECTION
150th anniversary bottling
Single Malt Scotch Whisky

This whisky has been bottled from a selected individual cask
in its natural state and shows the character of that cask.
It has not been diluted with water. It has not been treated to
change its colour and is free from all additives. It has
not been subjected to any filtration that might remove
natural constituents and spoil its flavour.
It is the authentic product of its distillery.

Bottled by Wm. Cadenhead, 32 Union Street, Campbeltown,
SCOTLAND

From
KINCLAITH
Distillery
Distilled March 1965 and bottled December 1989
Matured in an oak cask
for **24** years
70cl   Product of Scotland   51.4%vol

MALT	**Kinclaith**
DISTILLERY	Kinclaith
	Moffat Street, GLASGOW
OWNING COMPANY	Last licensed to Long John Distillers
PRODUCTION STATUS	Dismantled 1975
ESTABLISHED	1957-8

TASTING NOTES	18-year-old, 46%
NOSE	Light and smoky with a spirit sharpness.
TASTE	Full-bodied, smooth with an attractive finish.
COMMENTS	No longer with us and now in very limited supply. See page 155.

MALT	**Millburn**
DISTILLERY	Millburn
	⊟ INVERNESS, Inverness-shire
PRODUCTION STATUS	Closed 1985. Dismantled 1988
ESTABLISHED	c1807

TASTING NOTES	13-year-old, 46%
NOSE	A rich aroma with a faint sweetness.
TASTE	Full-bodied, a touch of fruit and a long finish.
COMMENTS	Sadly, the last distillery to close in Inverness but still available. See page 155.

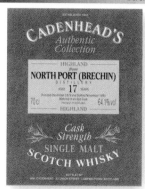

MALT	**North Port**
DISTILLERY	North Port
	BRECHIN, Angus
OWNING COMPANY	United Distillers
PRODUCTION STATUS	Closed 1983. No longer there
ESTABLISHED	c1820
SOURCE	Loch Lee

TASTING NOTES	1970, 40%
NOSE	A rather sharp, pronounced aroma, almost like a pickle.
TASTE	Starts sweet, but quickly fades to spirit — quite a sharp tang.
COMMENTS	Pre-dinner, with a little water. See page 155.

BRAND	**St Magdalene**
DISTILLERY	St Magdalene
	LINLITHGOW, West Lothian
OWNING COMPANY	United Distillers
PRODUCTION STATUS	Closed 1983. Converted into accommodation
ESTABLISHED	c1798
SOURCE	Loch Lomond

AGE WHEN BOTTLED	23 years
STRENGTH	58.1%

TASTING NOTES

NOSE	Fresh, light, oaky sweetness. Smoky and dry — a real pot pourri of enhancing aromas.
TASTE	Sweet at first, developing to a smooth, well-balanced dryness with a smoky flavour which finishes slowly but ripely.
COMMENTS	A splash of water is essential. An excellent dram.

CLOSED DISTILLERIES

MALT	**Benromach**
DISTILLERY	Benromach
	FORRES, Morayshire IV36 0EB
	01343-545111 01343-540155
OWNING COMPANY	Gordon & Macphail Ltd
PRODUCTION STATUS	Closed 1983. Currently being re-equipped by G&M
ESTABLISHED	1898
SOURCE	Chapelton Springs

TASTING NOTES	1970, 40%
NOSE	Light, delicate and attractive.
TASTE	Again, light and delicate but finishing with a pronounced taste of spirit.
COMMENTS	A pre-dinner dram from a distillery now owned by Gordon & Macphail. See page 154.

RARE MALTS
SELECTION

NATURAL
CASK STRENGTH
SINGLE MALT
SCOTCH WHISKY
AGED **22** YEARS
DISTILLED IN 1972 AT THE
BRORA
DISTILLERY
ESTABLISHED 1819
BRORA SUTHERLAND
58.7%vol 70cle
PRODUCE OF SCOTLAND
LIMITED BOTTLING

BRAND	**Brora**
DISTILLERY	Brora
	BRORA, Sutherland
OWNING COMPANY	United Distillers
PRODUCTION STATUS	Closed 1983. Will not reopen
ESTABLISHED	1819

AGE WHEN BOTTLED	22 years
STRENGTH	61.1%

TASTING NOTES

NOSE — Full, enthralling flavour, peaty and rich with a subtle sweetness.

TASTE — Rich, smooth with an abundance of nutty, smoky flavours which linger on with a memorable sweetness.

COMMENTS — After-dinner dramming of outstanding quality. Remember that splash of water though! Probably the most fully flavoured whisky outside Islay at the moment. Available as one of the UD Rare Malts Selection.

CONNOISSEURS CHOICE

Connoisseurs Choice, a range of single malts from various distilleries of Scotland.

The distillery situated in the area of the valley of the River Spey produce some of the finest malt whiskies.

SINGLE SPEYSIDE
MALT SCOTCH WHISKY

COLEBURN
DISTILLERY
Proprietors: J. & G. Stewart Ltd

DISTILLED 1972 DISTILLED

SPECIALLY SELECTED, PROCESSED AND BOTTLED BY
70cl   GORDON & MACPHAIL   40%vol
ELGIN · SCOTLAND
PRODUCT OF SCOTLAND

MALT	**Coleburn**
DISTILLERY	Coleburn
	Longmorn, ELGIN Morayshire
OWNING COMPANY	United Distillers
PRODUCTION STATUS	Closed 1985. Will not reopen
ESTABLISHED	1897
SOURCE	Spring in the Glen of Rothes

- -

TASTING NOTES	1972, 40%
NOSE	Light and flowery.
TASTE	Light and pleasant with a well-rounded refreshing aftertaste.
COMMENTS	Acquired by Distillers Company Ltd in 1930, it is representative of a typical small, two-still, late-Victorian distillery. See page 154.

MALT	**Convalmore**
DISTILLERY	Convalmore
	Dufftown, KEITH, Banffshire
OWNING COMPANY	Wm Grant & Sons Ltd
PRODUCTION STATUS	Closed 1985. Will not reopen
ESTABLISHED	1894
SOURCE	Springs in the Conval Hills

TASTING NOTES	1969, 40%
NOSE	Light, aromatic heather aroma.
TASTE	Much more on the palate than the nose suggests. A pleasant full roundness which drifts away slowly.
COMMENTS	An after-dinner malt from the old distillery. See page 154.

MALT	**Glenesk**
DISTILLERY	Glenesk
	🏠 Hillside, MONTROSE, Angus
OWNING COMPANY	United Distillers
PRODUCTION STATUS	Closed 1985. Will not reopen
ESTABLISHED	1897
SOURCE	River North Esk

AGE WHEN BOTTLED	12 years
STRENGTH	40%

TASTING NOTES	
NOSE	A light, delicate hint of sweetness.
TASTE	Quite full and sweet with a lingering finish, well balanced.
COMMENTS	After-dinner. The distillery was once known as North Esk and also as Hillside. Not an easy malt to find.

MALT	**Glenlochy**
DISTILLERY	Glenlochy
	🏠 FORT WILLIAM, Inverness-shire
OWNING COMPANY	United Distillers
PRODUCTION STATUS	Closed 1983. Will not reopen
ESTABLISHED	1898
SOURCE	River Nevis

TASTING NOTES	1974, 46%
NOSE	Light and aromatic.
TASTE	Light, spicy flavour which tends to finish quickly.
COMMENTS	Pre-dinner drinking but not for very much longer. See page 154.

BRAND	**Lochside**
DISTILLERY	Lochside
	📠 Brechin Road, MONTROSE
	Angus DD10 9AD
	☎ 01674-672737
OWNING COMPANY	Allied Domecq
PRODUCTION STATUS	Closed 1991
ESTABLISHED	1957
SOURCE	Borehole aquifer
MANAGER	Charles Sharpe
	🏠 2 🏠 2
AGE WHEN BOTTLED	10 years
STRENGTH	40%

- -

TASTING NOTES	
NOSE	Light, aromatic with a delicate sweetness and a gentle background of dryness.
TASTE	Initially sweet, medium/dry with a lingering, stimulating effect and a long, gentle finish
COMMENTS	Only available from the distillery office but well worth obtaining. This could become a collector's item.

MALT	**Port Ellen**
DISTILLERY	Port Ellen
	✉ PORT ELLEN, Islay, Argyll PA42 7AJ
OWNING COMPANY	United Distillers
PRODUCTION STATUS	Closed 1983. Will not reopen
ESTABLISHED	1825
SOURCE	Leorin Lochs

TASTING NOTES	1979, 40%
NOSE	A touch peat with a delicate, sweet bouquet.
TASTE	Quite full and round with hints of smoke and a smooth finish.
COMMENTS	A fine, underrated dram. Direct exports to the Americas were first pioneered at Port Ellen in the 1840s. The associated industrial maltings now supply a great deal of the island's malting requirement. See page 155.

Independent Bottlers

Many of the malts in this book are available from the two main Scottish independent bottlers although the stock varies according to when casks are drawn from the bond for bottling. If the malt you are looking for is not listed, it is best to call to confirm availability.

Gordon & MacPhail Ltd

George House
Boroughbriggs Road
ELGIN, Morayshire IV30 1JY
Tel: 01343-545111. Fax: 01343-540155
Gordon & MacPhail usually give the year of distillation instead of the age when bottled. Strength is normally 40% alcohol by volume.

Cadenheads Whisky Shop

172 Canongate
EDINBURGH EH8 8BN
Tel: 0131-556-5864.
Fax: 0131-556-2527 (retail & mixed cases)
Tel: 01586-554258 (wholesale)
William Cadenhead bottle malts at cask strength and these are unfiltered. Age varies depending on the cask being bottled. They still have substantial stock of their standard bottlings which are normally 46% alcohol by volume.

	G&M	Wm Cad
Aberfeldy	1975/77	
Ardbeg	1963/74	1975, 19 y.o.
Ardmore	1981	1977, 17 y.o.
Balblair	10 y.o, 1964	
Balmenach	1973/74	1981, 13 y.o.
Balvenie		1973, 21 y.o.
Banff	1974	1976, 17 y.o.

	G&M	**Wm Cad**
Ben Nevis		1977, 17 y.o.
Benriach	1980/81/82	1978, 17 y.o.
Benrinnes	1969/70	
Benromach	1971/72	1976, 18 y.o.
Bladnoch	1984/85	
Bowmore		1983, 12 y.o.
Brora	1972	1982, 13 y.o.
Bruichladdich	1964	1976, 18 y.o
Caol Ila	1980/81	1974, 20 y.o.
Caperdonich	1968/80/82	1977, 16 y.o.
Clynelish	12 y.o	1982, 12 y.o.
Coleburn	1972	
Convalmore	1969	1977, 17 y.o.
Cragganmore	1976/77/78	1982, 12 y.o.
Craigellachie	1974/77	
Dailuaine	1971/74	
Dallas Dhu	12 y.o.,1971	
Dalwhinnie	1970	
Deanston		1977, 17 y.o.
Dufftown		1966, 28 y.o.
Edradour		1976, 18&19 y.o.
Glen Albyn	1972/73	1964, 30 y.o.
Glenburgie	8 y.o, 1960/66/68/67/84	
Glencadam	1974	
Glencraig	1970	
Glen Elgin	1968	
Glenesk	1982	1982, 13 y.o.
Glenfarclas		1966, 28 y.o; 1980, 14 y.o.
Glenfiddich		1973, 21 y.o.
Glen Garioch		
Glenglassaugh	1983	
Glen Grant	21,25 y.o, 1936/48/49 50/51/52/54/59/60/63/65	1980, 14 y.o.
Glen Keith	1965/67	
Glenlivet	15,21 y.o, 1943/46/48 49/50/51/63/78	1980, 14 y.o.
Glenlochy	1977	1977, 17 y.o.
Glenlossie	1974/75	1978, 17 y.o.
Glen Mhor	8 y.o, 1963/65	1976, 18 y.o.
Glen Moray		1962, 32 y.o.
Glenrothes	8 y.o, 1956/57	
Glen Scotia		1977, 17 y.o

	G&M	Wm Cad
Glen Spey		1981, 13 y.o.
Glentauchers	1979	
Glenturret		1969, 25 y.o.
Glenugie	1966/67	
Highland Park	8 y.o, 1982	1977, 17 y.o; 1979, 15 y.o.
Imperial	1979	1979, 15 y.o
Inchmurrin		1985, 9 y.o.
Inverleven	1979/84	
Jura		1984, 10 y.o.
Kinclaith	1967/68	
Ledaig		1972, 22 y.o; 1973, 21 y.o.
Linkwood	15,21 y.o, 1939/46/54/61/68	1979, 15 y.o.
Lochside	1966	
Longmorn	12 y.o, 1956/63/64/69	
Macallan		1974, 20 y.o.
Macduff	1975	1978, 16 y.o
Mannochmore	1984	
Millburn	1971/72	1983, 11 y.o.
Milton Duff		1964, 30 y.o.
Mortlach	15,21 y.o, 1936/60/66	1987, 8 y.o.
Mosstowie	1975/79	
North Port	1974	1976, 17 y.o.
Old Elgin	8, 15 y.o, 1938/39/40/47	
Old Pulteney	8, 15 y.o, 1961	
Pittyvaich		1977, 16 y.o.
Port Ellen	1978/79/80 1981, 13 y.o; 1983, 12 y.o.	
Rhosdhu		1985, 9 y.o.
Rosebank	1983	
Royal Brackla		1972/74
Scapa	1984	
Speyburn	1971	1975, 19 y.o.
Springbank		1978, 16 y.o; 1985, 9 y.o.
St Magdalene	1966	1964, 30 y.o; 1982, 11&12 y.o.
Strathisla	21 y.o, 1948/49/54/55/58 60/63/67/72/80	
Talisker	1954/55	1979, 15 y.o; 1979, 14 y.o.
Tamdhu	8 y.o, 1957	1981, 13 y.o.
Tamnavulin		1973, 21 y.o.
Teaninich	1975/76/82	1983, 11 y.o.
Tomatin	1964/68	1976, 18 y.o.

The Keepers of the Quaich

The Keepers of the Quaich is an exclusive society established by the Scotch whisky industry to honour those around the world who have contributed greatly to the standing and success of Scotch whisky.

It also aims to build on the value and prestige of Scotch whisky internationally and to further interest in the lesser known aspects and attributes of the 'Spirit of Scotland'.

The organisation has members from 55 countries and includes leaders of the Scotch whisky industry and noted Scotch whisky connoisseurs and characters. All have one fundamental link in common — a love of Scotland and Scotch whisky. Under the patronage of (among others) His Grace, The Duke of Atholl, banquets are regularly held at Blair Castle in Perthshire to invest new members as Keepers and to promote not only Scotch but also Scotland. The seal of the society is therefore most appropriate — bestowed by the Lord Lyon, it proclaims UISGEBEAT-HA GU BRATH — Water of Life Forever.

FOUNDING PARTNERS

United Distillers

33 Ellersly Road
EDINBURGH EH12 6JW

United Distillers, the spirits company of Guiness plc, is the major producer of branded spirits in the UK with a portfolio of over 100 brands of Scotch whisky, gin, vodka and bourbon. UK sales are the responsibility of Perth-based United Distillers (UK) Ltd.

Allied Distillers Ltd

2 Glasgow Road
DUMBARTON G82 1ND

Incorporating George Ballantine & Son, William Teacher & Sons, Stewart & Son of Dundee and Long John International, this company formed in January 1988 controls the Scotch whisky interests of Allied-Domecq plc. Headquartered in Dumbarton, the company which operates two large grain distilleries and 12 malt distilleries, continues an association with the town first started in 1938 by Hiram Walker.

Justerini & Brooks Ltd

151 Marylebone Road
LONDON NW1 5QE

This company was founded in 1749 by Giacomo Justerini, an Italian cordial maker who came to London in pursuit of an Opera singer. He failed in his quest for the lady, but remained to form a commercial alliance with George Johnson and together they set themselves up as wine merchants. By 1760 the company had been granted the first of its eight successive Royal Warrants and in 1830 the company was bought by Alfred Brooks. A century later the house brand of Scotch — J&B Rare dominated the company's exports to the United States. After merging with Twiss Brownings and Hallowes to form United Wine Traders, the company bought Gilbeys in 1962 to form International Distillers and Vintners, now the drinks division of Grand Metropolitan PLC.

The Highland Distilleries Co plc

& Robertson & Baxter Ltd
106 West Nile Street
GLASGOW G1 2QY

The Highland Distilleries Company was incorporated in July 1887 as distillers of high quality malt whisky for the blending trade having secured the ownership of both Glenrothes and Bunnahabhain distilleries. Having acquired Glenglassaugh distillery in 1892 and Tamdhu in 1898, the company expanded its interests and later formed a close association with whisky brokers Robertson & Baxter Ltd. The malt portfolio was enlarged with the addition of Highland Park in Orkney in 1937 and its blended whisky interests were also furthered with the takeover of Matthew Gloag & Son Ltd, the Perth blenders of The Famous Grouse in 1970.

The Chivas & Glenlivet Division

The Seagram Company Ltd
111 Renfrew Road
PAISLEY PA3 4DY

In 1801 William Edward set up in business in Aberdeen as a wine and spirit merchant and grocer; he was joined some years later by James Chivas. They introduced Chivas Regal in the 1890's and this established their reputation within the trade. In 1949, Chivas Bros joined forces with Seagram's of Canada thus securing entry into the distilling world whilst strengthening their position in the trade. In 1950, they purchased

Strathisla Distillery and in 1957 Glen Keith was built. In the 1970s, Chivas commissioned two further distilleries — Braes of Glenlivet and Allt a' Bhainne. In 1978, Glenlivet Distillers joined the fold bringing four more distilleries into the portfolio — Glenlivet, Longmorn, Benriach and Caperdonich. The division is today responsible for all production, business development and global strategic planning for Seagram's Scotch whisky brands.

CORPORATE MEMBERS

Berry Bros & Rudd Ltd
   3 St James's Street
   LONDON SW1A 1EG

Burn Stewart Distillers PLC
   65 Kelburn Street
   GLASGOW G78 1LD

Campbell Distillers Ltd
   West Byrehill
   KILWINNING KA13 6LE

The Drambuie Liqueur Company Ltd
   Stirling Road
   KIRKLISTON
   West Lothian EH29 9EE

J&G Grant
   Glenfarclas Distillery
   Marypark
   BALLINDALLOCH
   Banffshire AB3 9BD

William Grant & Sons Ltd
   Independence House
   84 Lower Mortlake Road
   RICHMOND
   Surrey TW9 2HS

Inver House Distillers Ltd
   Towers Road
   AIRDRIE ML6 8PL

William Lawson Distillers Ltd
288 Main Street
COATBRIDGE ML5 3RH

Macallan-Glenlivet PLC
CRAIGELLACHIE
Banffshire AB3 9RX

Macdonald Martin Distilleries plc
186 Commercial Street
Leith
EDINBURGH EH6 6NN

Morrison Bowmore Distillers Ltd
Springburn Bond
Carlisle Street
GLASGOW G21 1EQ

The North British Distillery Co Ltd
Wheatfield Road
EDINBURGH
EH11 2PX

The Tomatin Distillery Co Ltd
TOMATIN IV13 7YT

The Whyte & Mackay Group PLC
Dalmore House
310 St Vincent Street
GLASGOW G2 5RG